PROOF *of* GOD

THE SHOCKING TRUE ANSWER

TO THE WORLD'S

MOST IMPORTANT QUESTION

Ptolemy Tompkins and Bernard Haisch

HOWARD BOOKS
AN IMPRINT OF SIMON & SCHUSTER, INC.

NEW YORK · LONDON · TORONTO · SYDNEY · NEW DELHI

Howard Books
An Imprint of Simon & Schuster, Inc.
1230 Avenue of the Americas
New York, NY 10020

First Howard Books trade paperback edition September 2017

HOWARD and colophon are trademarks of Simon & Schuster, Inc.

For information about special discounts for bulk purchases,
please contact Simon & Schuster Special Sales at 1-866-506-1949
or business@simonandschuster.com.

The Simon & Schuster Speakers Bureau can bring authors to
your live event. For more information or to book an event, contact
the Simon & Schuster Speakers Bureau at 1-866-248-3049 or visit
our website at www.simonspeakers.com.

Manufactured in the United States of America

10 9 8 7 6 5 4 3 2 1

Library of Congress Cataloging-in-Publication Data is available.

ISBN 978-1-5011-6154-4
ISBN 978-1-5011-6156-8 (ebook)

For Stuart Wing Ray and Emily Zinnemann—
strange bedfellows, united by the fact that without them,
this book would not exist.

—PTOLEMY TOMPKINS

I dedicate this to my wife, Marsha Sims, who supports and
inspires me every day and who spent many hours reading,
proofing, and copyediting. And thank you to my loving
family: Kate Haisch, Taylor Haisch, Elizabeth Henderson,
Jason Brenneman, Pamela Eakins, Joyce Eakins, and grandsons
Jamie and Will Brenneman, who are destined for greatness.

—BERNARD HAISCH

PART I

New York

CHAPTER 1

The Time Nyack

There are lots of nice things you can do with sand: but do not try building a house on it.

—C. S. LEWIS, *MERE CHRISTIANITY*

IN THE SUMMER of 2016, my wife Colleen and I had a falling out, and I suddenly found myself, with a few stray belongings, in a hotel at the edge of my town. A town in which I had lived for seven years, but that I was now dwelling in, essentially, as a stranger, for a little over one hundred dollars a night.

This change was painful but also fascinating. Seeing my town from the slight remove that sleeping in a strange bed at its outskirts provided, I realized that I didn't know the place at all.

The depression killed my appetite, and I often wouldn't get around to eating till sometime after midnight, when all the food stores and restaurants had closed. Walking down to the late-night convenience mart that was just a few blocks from my hotel, I'd feel like I was in a foreign country. I'd passed that convenience mart thousands of times driving home, but I'd never had occasion to go in before. The person working the counter (it always seemed to be a different person each night) would look at me like just another late-night traveler in off the highway that flowed past the hotel, headed from, and toward, who knows where.

Daytime was equally strange. The hotel—the Time Nyack—was a recent addition to the town, and had been built in the currently fashionable "boutique" style, which meant that it was supposed to be at once sophisticated yet cozy and personal. Make no mistake, the place was nice. However, it was situated in an abandoned mill between a freeway and a graveyard. My room was on the graveyard side, and my windows, though pleasantly large and tall like the room itself, looked directly onto a hill lined with twelve headstones.

These headstones would stare back at me like a slightly bored Greek chorus whenever I felt energetic enough to get up from bed and see what might be happening in the world outside.

The designers of the hotel had chosen, once again oddly to my mind, the figure of a skull as its central decorative motif. The first thing you saw when you walked inside the hotel was a large, decidedly ominous metal cutout of this logo on the wall by the check-in counter. Meanwhile, the carpet my bed sat on had a similar pair of skulls woven into it, one on each side of the bed, so that the one on the left (my side at home) was always the first thing my still-blurry eyes settled on when I swung my feet out of bed each morning.

When I left the hotel, which I did infrequently, the ill omens continued. Each time I turned the key in my car, my navigation system would helpfully tell me that I was just over half a mile from home. Had someone failed to tell it that this "home," while still existing in a physical sense, had ceased being home to me?

One afternoon, while I was driving down the main drag just outside town where all the chain and big-box stores were, a song from the early seventies, "Easy to Slip" by the group Little Feat, came on the radio. Most pop songs are, in one way or another, about heartbreak, and, as often happens in times of emotional distress, the words seemed directed straight at me that day. "All the people that you can't recall," sang Lowell George—although decades dead, clearly aware, somehow, of my current plight— "do they really exist at all?"

It was a good question. Did anything in this solid and predictable world we all moved through each day really and truly exist, or was it all just a lie, a big flowing river of sand, masquerading, for the moment, as solidity, reliability, permanence?

There was another reason those song lyrics hit me with such curious force that day. In the weeks leading up to my wife's and my split, I had been working with an astrophysicist named

Bernard Haisch on the beginnings of a book with the ambitious title *Proof of God*.

Several months back, I'd gotten an email from Haisch, who had just come back from a conference where he'd met an old friend of mine, the writer and researcher Stephan Schwartz. Bernie (as I soon came to call him) told Stephan that he'd written two books on what he considered to be very important—in fact, crucial—topics. He had, he said, a message he wanted to get out to the world.

Bernie's books had found readers, but not a "popular" audience. The reason for this was simple. Though fascinating, both books dealt with "heavy" subject matter. Despite Bernie's often heroic attempts to bring this subject matter down to the level of a common reader, neither of his two titles was the kind of thing someone might pick up on a whim at the airport. Perhaps, he asked, I would be interested in helping him retool these books so that they could reach a larger audience?

I had read Bernie's second book, *The Purpose-Guided Universe*, and been greatly impressed with its message. Bernie was a member of what I considered a very important minority group in the scientific community. He was a responsible, respected, accomplished scientist who believed, unapologetically, in God. The world, I felt, needed more scientists like this. And they needed to hear more from those that were already out there.

I did a little reading up on Bernie outside his books, and was reminded of something I'd read in *The Purpose-Guided*

Universe, that he had been instrumental in coming up with a controversial theory about what had at first struck me as an impossibly arcane subject: the generation of mass in the universe. In other words, how things, from bricks to baseballs to ball bearings, take on the solid, substantial feeling they have to us, when in fact (and as we shall shortly see in greater detail) all the seemingly solid objects around us are really made up completely of empty space and energy. Things appear to have mass, appear to be solid, to be *there,* Bernie explained to me, because of inertia.

> *He was a responsible, respected, accomplished scientist who believed, unapologetically, in God.*

What is inertia? In a nutshell, it's the tendency of things at rest to want to stay at rest.

"We experience inertia constantly," Bernie told me. "Any time a stationary object is forced to move it encounters inertia. It's why you need gas in your car if you want to drive it up a hill, and it's why it takes effort on your part to get up off the couch and grab another beer during game day. When you're on a plane and the pilot ups the throttle to prepare to take off, inertia is the force that pushes you back into your seat. The plane has suddenly started moving forward, and your body is attempting to stay at rest. But once you're up at thirty-five thousand feet going six hundred miles per hour, you don't feel the inertia anymore, because you are no longer accelerating; you are cruising along at a constant speed."

All solid matter encounters inertia when it speeds up. Inertia is the reason stuff in our world would rather hold still than move.

So what was so important about all this?

What was important, Bernie explained, is that though we know inertia creates the solid world, we don't know for sure just how it does this.

Four years before my conversation with Bernie, in 2013, Peter Higgs and his colleague François Englert had earned a Nobel Prize for their discovery of the so-called Higgs Particle—otherwise known as the Higgs Boson or, more spectacularly, as the "God Particle." Particles are, generally speaking, the smallest "things" in the universe. They're what those larger building blocks of our universe, protons and neutrons, are made of. (Electrons, much smaller than protons and neutrons, are themselves particles.) Each different kind of particle in the universe has a field associated with it. The discovery of the Higgs Particle was the big deal it was because once you've established that there is a Higgs Particle, it follows as a matter of course that there is a Higgs Field, as well. And it was the Higgs Field that had gotten scientists so excited, because it was postulated that this field caused friction, when particles moved against it, and created the illusion of mass in the universe. Without the Higgs Field, particles would have had nothing to push against, nothing to allow them, through the resistance caused by that Field, to generate the illusion of matter. No Higgs Field, no world. No wonder everyone had gotten so excited.

But here's where Bernie, and his two associates, Alfonso Rueda and Hal Puthoff, had come in. It was the opinion (not the certainty, Bernie stressed, but the opinion) that the solution put forth by Higgs and his associates might just not necessarily be correct after all.

"Might" was a word Bernie used constantly when we discussed this topic. It was extremely important to him that his colleagues not brand him what he called a "Higgs Denier." Science, it developed, was a touchy field, and a scientist's reputation could suffer enormously for one stray comment. Bernie had the highest respect for Higgs and the rest of the team that had created the breakthrough in possibly discovering the source of inertia. He just . . . wasn't entirely positive they were right. "Time," Bernie said, "will tell." This tendency to constantly qualify just about everything he said was one of the first indications I got that with Bernie I had found a genuine scientist. Responsible scientists, I realized, aren't interested in being right. They're interested in what *is* right. That, in the contentious world of the pro-God/anti-God debates that had been raging in the book world in recent years, was the kind of voice I thought people should hear more from.

I rolled all this around in my head. *A book about the reality of God's existence. Written with a scientist. One who incidentally just might turn out to have a viable alternative theory on the creation of mass, the phenomenon that lies behind the apparent solidity of our universe.*

This didn't sound like such a bad idea for a book to me.

And who knows, I thought, maybe I was the one to write it. Four years earlier, I'd played a part in helping Dr. Eben Alexander produce his bestseller about his near-death experience, *Proof of Heaven*. On the strength of my part in that book, the year before, I'd written a book called *Proof of Angels* with a Utah policeman named Tyler Beddoes, about the rescue of an eighteen-month-old baby, Lily Groesbeck, from an overturned car, and the mysterious voice that Tyler and three other officers had heard as they struggled to right the car. They'd all heard a voice that, they discovered when the car was once again right-side-up, had come from nowhere. The only other person in the car besides Baby Lily was her mother, Jennifer Groesbeck, who, the officers quickly realized, had died on impact some twelve hours earlier.

Far from having disproved God's existence, science has increasingly shown that God is, in fact, the best explanation so far found for the universe and everything in it.

A surgeon who travels beyond his body while in a coma. A policeman who hears a strange voice from a car from which no voice could rationally come. And, rounding things out . . . an astrophysicist who believed in God.

I told Bernie I wasn't up for retooling his previous books.

They were, it seemed to me, just fine the way they were. But I did want to collaborate on an all-new book with him: one that would burn his message down to its very basics, so that someone with not a lot of time or scientific background could pick the book up, read it fast, and absorb what, to my mind, was a crucial and hugely empowering message: Science is not a barrier to faith, but an aid to it. Far from having disproved God's existence, science has increasingly shown that God is, in fact, the best explanation so far found for the universe and everything in it.

One of science's most beloved principles is something called Occam's razor. Named for the fourteenth-century Franciscan philosopher William of Occam, this rule states that the simplest explanation is usually the best. If you have a no-nonsense, straightforward explanation for something, and a hugely convoluted, complex, and just plain unlikely one, Occam's razor states that you are probably better off going for the simpler one, as it's more likely to be true. As Bernie would show me again and again, when it came to the universe, the things in it, and the way those things work, the simplest and best explanation really and truly is: "God did it."

Named for the fourteenth-century Franciscan philosopher William of Occam, this rule states that the simplest explanation is usually the best.

Most science today is strongly reductionist. That means it closely follows the principle of Occam's razor, opting relentlessly for the simple over the complex, the right-in-front-of-you over the mystifying and far-flung.

Or at least, that's its reputation. But as Bernie was to show me, when the idea of God's possible existence came up, most scientists promptly dropped Occam's razor like a hot potato. Instead of a simple and straightforward explanation, they'd opt for some other, often ridiculously convoluted counter-explanation. God, for any person who truly valued science, could not possibly be an explanation for anything.

In just about all the current arguments about the universe and how it came to be, "God did it" is the best and easiest explanation. Yet this has been consistently covered up by mainstream scientific publications.

Not only that, but all of these *no-God-allowed* counter-explanations were 100 percent hypothetical. There was not a shred of evidence for any of them. And yet, in spite of this, they received huge play in the mainstream media. Why? Because many scientists, and popular writers in general, had an agenda to keep God out of science at all costs.

If there's one thing that's unscientific, it's an agenda. True science is supposed to be absolutely open to the facts as they stand. Yet when the facts as they stand pointed toward a God who had created the universe, those facts were buried, ignored, or ridiculed, while far-less-likely explanations for the universe being the place it is, were held up in their place.

Though it's not supposed to be, science, in short, is political. In just about all the current arguments about the universe and how it came to be, "God did it" is the best and easiest explanation. Yet this has been consistently covered up by mainstream scientific publications—even though this is grossly unscientific behavior.

Most books have a selfish motive at work somewhere in them—usually right at the surface. I was, and had for a long time, been very interested in science's attitude toward God, and in particular in mainstream science's tendency to push Him out of the picture. Like every member of modern society, I had spent my whole life in a world ruled by two dueling masters, each constantly fighting to achieve dominance. On one side was "science," and on the other was "faith." And like a child growing up in a household where the parents can't get through a single evening without fighting, I was tired of it.

Yet I also knew this argument could not go on forever. Sooner or later, one side would win. Unless . . . this angry couple finally gave up and went to a counselor. If they did, perhaps they would learn what believing scientists like Bernie had been arguing for some time now. True science, and true religion, could not possibly be at odds with each other. For in fact, true science and true religion obeyed the same master, and it was what that master had to say that really mattered.

Who was this master—this authority who, if consulted, would level all the tiresome and increasingly strident arguments between science and religion instantly null and void?

That authority was Truth.

> *True science, and true religion, could not possibly be at odds with each other. For in fact, true science and true religion obeyed the same master, and it was what that master had to say that really mattered.*

Truth, the real voices of wisdom have argued again and again over the centuries, is like a mountain. It may be approached from different directions, and the paths to its peak may vary from the extremely roundabout to the devastatingly direct. But whichever route you take, truth is a mountain with *one peak*. If a mountain has one peak, and all the paths on that mountain lead upward, then sooner or later, all those paths will end up at the same place.

Bernie was a scientist who believed in God. As such, he embodied in one person two styles of thinking about the world that many people thought were destined forever to be mutually exclusive.

But if truth was single, science and faith eventually had to meet on equal footing, and had to get along when they did so. Perhaps Bernie held the key to a question I had been curious about all my adult life. If so, then I was all ears.

CHAPTER 2

God and Me—A Brief History

I SPENT MOST OF my childhood in McLean, Virginia, and from second through ninth grade went to an exceptionally upscale institution called the Potomac School.

Potomac is an Episcopal school, and it was at Potomac that God, or at least a certain version of God, and I were first formally introduced. This was a God of weekly church services, a God who was the subject of quiet, but generally not too passionate belief, and a God who got along well with science because He simply stayed quiet and opted not to pick a fight.

In the fifth-grade Christmas play, I was assigned the role of Augustus Caesar. The curtain opened, and I strode onstage, eyeing the audience of parents, teachers, and hapless visiting relatives dragged to the school gym with a cold and merciless scorn. Identifying myself ("My name, Augustus Caesar is!"),

I bragged for a bit about my unassailable power and influence over the world in all directions, and then proclaimed that I would be demanding a tax ("Each man shall one penny pay!" etc.). I then strode offstage, only appearing again at the play's end, when—in a neat and tidy, if unhistorical, wrap-up to the action—I gave the newborn savior my blessings.

During my years at Potomac, my own relationship with God—or with the being who seemed to stand behind the clues about Him given us at school—was a fairly chilly one. For there was no getting around the fact that the Episcopalian version of God being foisted on us at Potomac was exceedingly dull. So dull that, in the last analysis, the question of whether or not He actually existed didn't really seem to matter. After all, what was this bloodless, watery abstraction, this vague, somewhat benevolent spook hovering off behind the scenes somewhere, compared to dinosaurs, or horror comics, or sharks, or, some time later on, girls?

Not that, most of the time, this lack of interest on my part presented much of a problem. God was boring, but that was okay because—Christmas play aside—He just didn't come up that much.

But there *were* exceptions to this, the chief among them being the Lord's Prayer.

From second grade through ninth, I, along with the rest of Potomac's students, recited this prayer each day at morning assembly. This was always mildly tedious. But at some point—

I have no memory exactly when—it became *more* than tedious. When the Lord's Prayer was said, I quietly mumbled a sort of alternative, protest edition of it. I don't remember exactly how it went, but it was something along these lines:

Our Father, who doesn't exist
I don't care if I'm supposed to believe in you.
I don't, you are a phony,
and no one can make me say different
Because I know better.

Why this animosity on my part? Why, given what a small imposition on my time and attention this prayer made, did I go to the trouble of quietly reciting this alternative to it?

Because, it gradually emerged, I *did* care about God after all. I cared about Him enormously, in fact. My problem with this Lord's Prayer business was—though I wouldn't have used this word at the time—its lack of any kind of *organic* feel. There was just nothing real about it. If there was something big at work in life, some genuine director lurking far back there, out of sight but in charge all the same, this nameless entity was clearly not the dull and bloodless abstraction to which we Potomac students were forced to pay daily allegiance.

God—*my* God—was something different altogether. He was an entity having to do, chiefly, with nature: with sharks, with wolves, with the ocean, with that funny charged feeling that the air took on just before a big thunderstorm arrived, and, most important, with a certain strange and nameless feeling of mystery and vastness that would come over me, and had been coming over me, now and then, for as long as I could remember.

What was the specific nature of this feeling, and how did it fit in with what I knew of the world? Well, that was just it. I didn't know. All I knew was that this feeling, which would stop me in my tracks at odd moments and overwhelm me with a feeling of distance and mystery and possibilities unknown—possessed precisely what the God of those morning school assemblies so completely lacked:

Reality.

When I hit adolescence, my obsession with the natural world intensified. I would look for hours on end through my animal books, studying the shape of a shark's fin, or the slick, strangely hypnotic gloss on the fur of an otter.

Something in nature at its most beautiful and big made me desperately and wonderfully homesick for something.

This feeling for the strange, indefinable *rightness* of the natural world only intensified when I put my books down and entered the natural world myself. I found there a sparkle and pulse—an indefinable feeling of life that was *more* than simply life. Whatever this thing I sensed was, it struck a strange note not just of admiration or appreciation but of . . . recognition. Something in nature at its most beautiful and big made me desperately and wonderfully homesick for something. Yet what and where this Something was, I didn't know.

In short, though I wouldn't have described it this way at the time, the older I got the more I saw nature through a spiritual lens.

At the same time, I was becoming more unhappy with the way the natural world was presented to me in the Science classes I was taking at school, and in the books I found in the Nature section of bookstores. When I opened a book on animals that was too dense with scientific facts (the gestation period of marsupials versus that of more modern mammals; the migration patterns of this or that species of waterfowl), I'd feel like I'd been subjected to a kind of bait and switch. I had opened the book to learn something about animals or birds or fish. The problem was that I didn't know what, exactly, I wanted to learn. All I did know was that it had nothing to do with breeding seasons or population densities, or even (though this was slightly more interesting) with animal behavior. It had, in short, nothing to do with data of any sort. It had to do with something else: a something else that I became ever more drawn to as my teenage years passed, even as I remained ignorant of its true nature.

Meanwhile, I continued my reading. And as I did so, I began to run into a different kind of nature book. These books, written by people like Henry Beston, Loren Eiseley, and Farley Mowat, did more than simply describe the natural world. They also sought to describe that sense of mystery and wonder that emanated from it. Henry Beston seemed to sum up this vision of nature as well as anyone.

"We need," wrote Beston in his book *The Outermost House,* "another and a wiser and perhaps a more mystical concept of animals. . . . They are not brethren, they are not underlings; they are other nations, caught with ourselves in the net of life and time, fellow prisoners of the splendor and travail of the earth."

It wasn't long after I discovered these kinds of writers that I discovered poetry: not the vaguely pious and annoying poems I would occasionally be forced to read at school, but a more direct, potent, and (often) mystically inclined variety. One which seemed to focus directly on the spiritual component at work in nature, and what that component might mean. "We dance round in a ring and suppose," wrote Robert Frost, a "nature" poet who was also clearly a poet of the mystery that hid within and behind nature, "but the Secret sits in the middle and knows."

Growing up, I spent a lot of summers and holidays on the South Fork of Long Island. The water off Long Island is cold all year. It warms up a bit in summer, but only a bit. The waves, on the best days, were big and rude and rough, and marching through them to get to deeper water took effort and persistence. When I would go to the beach with my father and stepmother and whatever other adults were around, they would enter the water swiftly and briefly. They'd tiptoe out, sink down to their necks, then rush back to the sand, ready for more sunbathing, more reading of the *New York Times*, more boring, adult-style talk.

I wanted none of this. When we got to the beach, I would immediately throw my towel to the sand and march off into the surf. The colder and rougher it was, the better.

The cold was unpleasant at first, but that was part of the process. Step after deliberate step, I'd march out through the incoming army of waves until the water was deep enough for me to plunge beneath the next one that rolled in.

This initial plunge always delivered a shock to my system, but the next one would be easier. Finally, I'd make it out to the precise point where the waves began to break. Now, instead of having to plunge and duck beneath the next incoming wave, I could keep my head out of the water and jump over it.

By this time, my body was so immune to the cold that the frigid, churning water around me lost all its sting and became warm as a relaxing bath. Big waves usually came intermittently, in sets of three or so. When I saw a big one forming out in the water beyond, I'd wait till the wave was almost upon me and the water level suddenly dropped. For a moment, my feet would brush the sandy bottom. I'd push hard, and as the wall of water swept toward me I would rise, up and up and up, till the peak hit, and I had a sudden, brief, glorious view of everything around me.

Sometimes, when a big wave came in and swept me up like that, I'd turn as I rose so that, at the moment when the wave was at its highest, I was looking back toward land. When that happened I'd sometimes get a quick, satisfying glimpse of the adults back on shore. There they'd be, those poor, distant schlubs, sitting there with their *New York Times* and their sun lotion and their apples and cheese, while *I* was out where it mattered, where things were going on. Where the energy was.

The more sophisticated my reading got, the more voices I found who knew, and described, just what I would feel out there in the waves on days like that.

"What is this that frees me so in storms?" asked Walt Whitman. Ralph Waldo Emerson, in his famous essay "Nature," described how sometimes just being in the woods alone could transform his thinking: "Crossing a bare common, in snow puddles, at twilight, under a clouded sky, without having in my thoughts any occurrence of special good fortune, I have enjoyed a perfect exhilaration. I am glad to the brink of fear. . . . Standing on the bare ground . . . all mean egotism vanishes. I become a transparent eye-ball; I am nothing; I see all; the currents of the Universal Being circulate through me; I am part or parcel of God."

Except, as both Whitman and Emerson of course knew, it wasn't nature these poets and writers were entering, or at least not *just* nature. There was something else out there in the waves and woods as well. Something I couldn't quite put my finger on, yet knew, all the same, was real. Nature, for writers like Emerson or Whitman, was clearly a place where something more was to be found—a "something" I found described not just by Americans, but with equally stunning clarity in lines like these by the nineteenth-century British poet William Wordsworth:

A sense sublime
Of something far more deeply interfused,
Whose dwelling is the light of setting suns,
And the round ocean and the living air,
And the blue sky, and in the mind of man

In addition to Long Island, I was lucky enough to be able to spend some time, most summers, on an island off the coast of Maine called Islesboro.

On the south end of Islesboro there is a small community called Dark Harbor. Dark Harbor is what's called a summer colony—in other words, a collection of big, fancy houses that wealthy folk come up to and inhabit for a month or two, before they disappear back to New York, or Boston, or whatever similar place they came from. I'd been coming to Dark Harbor with my father and mother since I was a baby, and consequently felt an even stronger sense of identity with the place than I did with Long Island (which I'd only started visiting in the seventies, when my stepmother came along).

In the short but intense summer season, status—who you were, who you were related to, how much money you had—counted for a lot on Islesboro, and the adults made little secret of just how important all this stuff was to them. During my late teens, when I'd go up there with a little more insight into the whys and wherefores of adult behavior, I'd always be amazed at how miserable most of the people there were. They seemed to ignore the beauty of the place and spend all their time jockeying for social position.

The land and the water in Dark Harbor had a strange, unnamable intensity—one that some places just have more of than others. I'd take long walks by myself, past all the giant summer houses, down to the southern tip of the island to watch the sun set, or just sit on an empty rocky shore staring out at the other islands set in the cold, black current of Penobscot Bay. I'd get that same feeling I'd get in the water when I was down on Long Island. *I have the secret*, I'd think to myself. *I don't know what that secret is, but I know that I have it, and I know that if I am careful, and hold on to it, nothing will ever be able to take it away from me.*

Again, the new writers I was regularly discovering, and most especially the poets, only intensified this feeling.

"Whose woods these are I think I know," Robert Frost wrote in "Stopping by Woods on a Snowy Evening," and I knew exactly what Frost was getting at with those lines. The woods, the ocean—these wild, weird, necessary, supremely energizing places—were most often owned by wealthy people. People who had no clue what was really going on in them. But there were other people who did know, who felt the strong, unquestionable magic at work in them, and knew that that magic meant something.

But the older I got, the harder it became for me to get this feeling—at least without help. For all my twenties and the first part of my thirties, I drank quite a bit. For most of this time, my absolute favorite thing to do was to get really drunk and then throw myself—literally—into nature. One day down in Florida, in a small beach town just south of Fort Lauderdale called Dania, I drank an entire bottle of rum while floating around in the waves. When I finished it, I ran up onto the beach, responsibly deposited the empty bottle in a trashcan, then ran back into the water.

"I think I'm going to go out for a bit," I said to my girlfriend Sarah, who'd been floating around with me. "I might be a while but I'll be back."

With that, I swam, and swam, and swam, heading directly away from the coast.

Behind me as I swam, the sun moved slowly toward the western horizon. Before I knew it, the last little bit of it had vanished out of sight, and the formerly blue sky above me had turned a deep, vaguely melancholy shade of purple. The first stars started to appear, and the next time I turned my head toward shore a friendly little string of lights had snapped on in the darkness, seemingly in answer to the stars in the sky above.

Admiring the beauty of the scene, I couldn't help noticing that the friendly little line of lights twinkling at me from shore was considerably far away. Well, I'd wanted to get away from things, out into the wild, and it was looking like I'd succeeded.

Swimming back to shore would have been the prudent move at this point. But it was also the easy one, and as I was still quite drunk, I decided to linger a little longer out there in the dark and the space.

But I didn't just float there. Instead, I repeatedly took big lungfuls of air, ducked my head under the water, and swam hard straight down. When I got as deep as I could, I stopped and floated there, upside down in the blackness, holding as still as I could. I was a good half mile from land, it was dark, and it was not impossible that there might be a shark or three in the area, especially as sharks typically moved in from deeper water at dusk to hunt along the shore. But suspended there in the dark, far from the ordinary, humdrum world, I felt no fear at all. Instead, a strange but familiar joy shot through me. I was, once again, close to that thing-that-was-not-a-thing, that realm of mystery and strangeness that was, paradoxically, not strange and distant but close. It was so close, and so obvious and intimate, that every time I once again brushed up against it, I'd marvel that I could ever have lost it. Being eaten by a shark was, I thought, a small price to pay for such a feeling.

Sooner or later, with the rum beginning to wear off, I determined that it was time to head back to shore.

Managing this, however, proved tougher than I'd thought. Not only was the land considerably farther away than I'd thought, but I was also having a hard time figuring out just which cluster of lights to aim for.

At around nine o'clock, I finally staggered out of the water onto the same beach I'd left some three hours earlier. Sarah, greatly relieved to see me, ran a little way up the beach to a payphone and made a call to the Coast Guard.

"They were on their way," she said, "because I was starting to think you weren't coming back."

But I always came back. Still, as the years progressed and my drinking increased, it began to seem less certain that I really wanted to. One Fourth of July out in San Diego, where I moved with Sarah, I decided on a daytime ocean excursion from the beach in Coronado, which lay just over a causeway from San Diego proper.

After about an hour's leisurely swimming, I stopped to look back at the coast, and saw, off in the distance, something surprising. A swimmer was cutting through the water directly toward me.

As the swimmer got closer, I could see he was towing one of those small, red, bullet-shaped flotation devices such as one saw on *Baywatch*. A lifeguard.

Uh-oh, I thought. *I've done it now.*

In what seemed to me like an extraordinarily short time, the lifeguard, towing that red bullet behind him, made it out to where I was.

"How you doing?" he asked cheerfully, and not in the least out of breath.

"Fine," I said.

"You're out pretty far. You sure you're all right?"

"Oh yeah," I said, hoping that he was sufficiently far away that he couldn't smell the alcohol on my breath. "Am I in trouble or something?"

"Heck no," the lifeguard said, then laughed. "This is America. Land of the free. Especially," he added, "on the Fourth of July."

And with that, he turned and resumed his powerful, steady crawl, cutting back to shore with the same marvelous speed and sureness with which he'd gotten out to me.

He's right, I thought, alone again out there in the blue, my country spread out before me like some vast Fourth of July beach blanket. *I can do anything I want. I wonder . . . just what it is I want to do.*

Though I'd just finished my first book, on Mesoamerican religion, and it had been published by a good publisher, I was barely scraping by in life, teaching English at a third-rate San Diego language school and getting helped with my meager monthly expenses by two hundred dollars sent every month by my sister and brother-in-law. I may have felt free out there in the ocean that Fourth of July. But back on land, life was plainly getting the better of me. And, sad to admit, free as it could still make me feel at times, close as it could still get me to that source of mystery and strangeness I so longed and lived for, most of the time my drinking wasn't really helping matters either.

It was shortly after that Fourth of July encounter out in the ocean that I happened to read a short book by C. S. Lewis called *Surprised by Joy*. The book—a memoir of Lewis's early days—is also a wonderfully roundabout yet at the same time curiously direct story of how Lewis came to accept the Christian faith.

Early on in the book, I came across a sequence that stopped me in my tracks as few passages have before or since. In the passage, Lewis is talking about the imaginary world he lived in as a child—one which struck me as deeply and instantly familiar, for it was the same world I myself had inhabited back then.

The passage caused me to remember when, at around eight years old, I felt the easy, comforting bath of imagination that I'd been immersed in for the first years of my life suddenly begin to drain away. This moment, when the plug is pulled on the womb-like safety of one's childhood imaginary world, is instantly familiar to many people—and many parents. It's the moment when children stop talking to their toys—when, while they're alone in the bath or their room, you no longer hear them having animated conversations. It's the moment when a kind of curtain comes down between the child and a world that he or she had never imagined would disappear . . . but now does.

When this happened to me, I remember vowing, sometime around age eight, never to forget that this world was *real*, and always would be. Though I could no longer see it clearly, I told myself to remember that it was always present, always right there, whether I could feel it or not.

The memory of that feeling of sureness about the existence of a spiritual world that I'd experienced so strongly up to the age of eight was, of course, one reason why I'd eventually found myself unable to say the Lord's Prayer at Potomac. Yet even as I'd grown into an adult appreciation of the spiritual dimension as it manifested in other cultures, I'd kept my distance from Christianity.

Until Lewis, a devout Anglican, began to bring me back toward it. It was Lewis who succeeded in making, for me, the supremely unlikely connection between that realm of mystery I had so long been familiar with and the religion into which I had been born.

His key to doing so was also about as unlikely as one could imagine. Lewis brought me face-to-face with Christianity through Beatrix Potter's children's book *The Tale of Squirrel Nutkin*.

"Though I loved all the Beatrix Potter books," Lewis wrote in *Surprised by Joy*, "the rest of them were merely entertaining; it [*The Tale of Squirrel Nutkin*] administered the shock, it was a trouble. It troubled me with what I can only describe as the idea of Autumn. It sounds fantastic to say that one can be enamored of a season, but that is something like what happened. . . . The experience was one of intense desire. And one went back to the book, not to gratify the desire . . . but to reawake it."

In looking at the book, Lewis experienced "surprise" and a "sense of incalculable importance. It was something quite different from ordinary life and even from ordinary pleasure; something, as they would say now, 'in another dimension.'"

In a few lines, Lewis had gone to the very heart of a childhood experience that I'd thought was altogether beyond the reach of words. But not only that: He had connected that experience (for as the book developed, it became clear that this was the true source of the sense of "incalculable importance" he had brushed up against) with the seemingly exterior story of a man who had lived and died two thousand years ago. A story that, up to then, I'd thought had nothing to do with me.

The barrier to Christianity that had stood since those long-ago days on the assembly-room floor of my elementary school broke down. And in the ensuing years, I came more and more to see that the mystery at the heart of Christianity was that same mystery I'd felt as a child and a teenager, and that I'd vowed never to lose.

Further revelations—usually packaged, craftily, in the form of disasters—followed. In 1995, when my drinking finally came to a head and I found myself in rehab, I was presented with a copy of *Alcoholics Anonymous*, otherwise known as the Big Book.

At first, I had no interest in reading the thing. But, lacking any other fare to help pass the hours, I finally broke down and started in on it.

It was Chapter Three, "We Agnostics," that held what was, for me, the revelatory passage.

"Lack of power, that was our dilemma. We had to find a power by which we could live, and it had to be A Power Greater Than Ourselves. Obviously. But where and how were we to find this Power? . . . We looked askance at many individuals who claimed to be godly. How could a Supreme Being have anything to do with it all? And who could comprehend a Supreme Being anyhow? Yet, in other moments, we found ourselves thinking, when enchanted by a starlit night, 'Who, then, made all this?' There was a feeling of awe and wonder, but it was fleeting and soon lost. Yes, we of agnostic temperament have had these thoughts and experiences. Let us make haste to reassure you. We found that as soon as we were able to lay aside prejudice and express even a willingness to believe in a Power greater than ourselves, we commenced to get results, even though it was impossible for any of us to fully define or comprehend that Power, which is God."

Sure, the language was a little goofy, a little dated. And yet I knew immediately what this passage was getting at. That strange sense of atmosphere and mystery, that feeling of getting to the secret at the heart of the world. A secret that, in childhood, nature had handed over without question, and that back in the good old early days of my drinking, had still been in reach.

Here, in a book that I'd expected to be full of tiresome do-good admonishments, was that same feeling, that same instinct for something larger. And far from being scorned or denied, it was being celebrated.

That one passage made all the difference for me. Apparently going along with this not-drinking thing would not mean I had to give up my belief in that larger, secret thing I'd been so taken up with all my life. Not only that, but this new perspective made it clear to me, for perhaps the first time, that my entire drinking career had, in fact, been devoted to pursuing it.

Alcoholics like me were all, when you got down to it, after the same thing: that thing was God.

Up to this point I'd had little interest in stopping drinking, or in absorbing any of the directives that my supervisors at rehab were so anxious to shove down my throat. But this passage, and what it so easily and honestly suggested, changed my thinking. It was so simple. Alcoholics like me were all, when you got down to it, after the same thing: that thing was God.

Of course, the AA literature was quick to point out that the "higher power" one needed to focus on in order to move beyond the compulsion to drink didn't *have* to be God, and there was plenty of assurance in the meetings I attended, both in rehab and afterward, that if one felt dicey about the God business, one only needed to select a "higher power" of some other sort, and focus one's recovery on that.

But I didn't need any of that. I knew full well what my "higher power" was. It was that same presence that had been hovering just behind the scenes my whole life. You could call it what you wanted, perhaps, but I knew its name was God.

When I got out of rehab, I did some more reading around in the history of AA, and discovered something very interesting. Bill Wilson, the cofounder of AA, had received key inspirations for AA from two authors I admired, but that I'd had no idea had played a part in AA's birth.

These two men were William James, the pioneering psychologist and philosopher and author of the classic book *The Varieties of Religious Experience*, and the Swiss psychologist Carl Jung.

Alcoholics, I learned from Wilson via Jung, were on what Jung called a "low-level" religious quest. They drank not because there was something innately wrong or weak in their natures, but because they sought God. The desire to drink, Jung wrote to Wilson, was, in Jung's opinion, "the equivalent, on a low level, of the spiritual thirst of our being for wholeness, expressed in medieval language: the union with God."

Jung quoted the first line from Psalm 42:

"As the hart panteth after the water brooks, so panteth my soul after thee, O God." These were astonishingly simple, straightforward words, but they were also the first thing anyone had ever told me about my own drinking that made real sense of it. They were the first things that explained to me that what I'd really been seeking with alcohol, and at stray moments brushing up against, were those same feelings that had come to me so easily as a child, less easily as a teenager, and finally all but impossibly as an adult.

Throughout all of these experiences, and these sudden, stunning passages from books, certain words were appearing again and again. "Freedom." "Wholeness." And another, one that I would not see the full implications of until I met Bernie:

"Consciousness."

CHAPTER 3

The Astronomer-Priest

BERNIE HAISCH WAS born in Germany, but his family moved
to Indianapolis, Indiana, in 1952, when he was three. Four
years previously, in 1948, Bernie's aunt and her husband had
moved to Indiana to escape life in postwar Germany, which in
the years immediately following the war was intensely bleak.
Bernie's aunt wrote long letters to Bernie's mother telling her
what a wonderland America was. So Bernie and his parents
took off from Genoa, Italy, on a steamer bound for the Land of
Opportunity.

Bernie's aunt told his mother of a bakery near their home
that was for sale. Bernie's mother and father could buy it, she
said, and carve out a piece of the American dream for themselves.

The bakery, however, turned out to be a mirage (or, as

Bernie likes to put it, "half-baked"), and Bernie's parents found themselves stuck in a new country where they didn't speak the language very well and had few prospects for work. The Haisches moved into a small two-bedroom apartment near downtown Indianapolis. The neighborhood was, as Bernie told me, "fairly low-class, but terrific compared to Germany."

After several weeks, Bernie's dad got a job at a custom aluminum metal products company where, to his surprise, most of the employees spoke German, so he didn't have to worry about learning the troublesome language of his new country. Meanwhile Bernie's mother turned their apartment into a comfortable home, joined the local Catholic church, and set herself to becoming an American.

Bernie's earliest memory from America is of being on a pedal car when he was about four. "I'd pedaled off the beaten track, into a stretch of woodland," he told me. "At least that's what it felt like at the time. It was probably just an undeveloped plot of land—a place with no houses on it yet, though there soon would be. I got scared, and I started calling out, 'Mamma, Mamma!'"

Bernie's mother was in their apartment, way out of earshot, but somehow she picked up on Bernie's situation and ran to his aid. You might say this was Bernie's introduction to what scientists call action at a distance: the phenomenon of one object affecting another without any apparent means of doing so. It would turn out to be a subject that Bernie spent a lot of time thinking about in the future.

Bernie also has a memory of playing in a sandbox with a car that he decided, in that strange, instantaneous, and unarguable way that imaginative children do, was not a car at all. It was a space vehicle, moving through the ghostly white dunes of the moon.

"Those early childhood years of mine," he told me, "were the start of the real heyday of excitement about space. For a lot of people these days, it's hard to understand just how exciting it all was back then. When Sputnik, the first Russian satellite, went up in October of 1957, I was in third grade. It was, of course, too bad the Russians did it instead of us, but it was still a miracle. A new world was opening up right above our heads, and for me it all seemed so close that I could almost reach out and touch it."

After school, Bernie watched a program called *Rocky Jones, Space Ranger.* "It was pretty hokey stuff from today's perspective. Cardboard sets, ridiculous costumes, planets clearly made from Styrofoam. But I loved it. I imagined myself traveling through space at the helm of my own personal rocket ship, just like Rocky Jones did, joystick in hand. Looking at the moon on clear nights, it just felt so *close*. Space was this whole vast new domain, a new world waiting to be explored. And I could be one of those explorers."

When Bernie was eight, he started drawing his own comic book series: *Bernard Haisch, Space Cadet.* He put his brother and cousins in the stories, exploring space, finding new worlds. As a young teen, he read a lot of science fiction. But in spite of the plentiful films he saw and comic books he read featuring malevolent, multi-armed, laser-eyed aliens, for Bernie the universe was, from the very beginning, a distinctly friendly place.

"For me as a kid, space was not some harsh wasteland, but close and approachable: a place that was basically beckoning to us. It was, in a way, what the computer world has become for so many of today's kids. The place where new worlds were to be found, new adventures were to be had. You could almost say it had a kind of holiness to it. It was a true *frontier*. Alpha Centauri, our nearest star next to the sun, was just four light-years away. Well—" Bernie stopped himself, making what I soon came to recognize as a characteristic correction. "Actually Proxima Centauri is a little closer. But the point is that these bodies were out there, we knew how far away they were, and they were screaming to us to be learned about. People need a sense of wonder—a sense of larger worlds yet to be seen. They wither up and die without it. Space, back then, delivered that sense."

> *"For me as a kid, space was not some harsh wasteland, but close and approachable: a place that was basically beckoning to us."*

Bernie knew by first grade that he wanted to be an astronomer. Stars were Bernie's first love, and the desire to study them stayed with him through high school. Bernie's mom was a devout Catholic, and the Haisch household had a strong religious atmosphere. But instead of jettisoning the Catholicism of his youth as he grew older, Bernie saw himself as combining his mother's faith with his wonder at the stars into a single, contradiction-free package.

"You could almost say it had a kind of holiness to it."

"There are some things," he writes in *The God Theory*, "that you just know—especially as a child, when your world is not yet filled with the ambiguities and doubts that grow and haunt you later in life."

"I knew I wanted to study space from basically as early as I can remember," Bernie told me. "I can't remember a time when the stars and planets—and especially the stars—weren't calling to me to study them. But my early memories are also about the house, the atmosphere, that I grew up in. And that was a house, and an atmosphere, saturated with Catholicism. My mother was a deeply religious person, and pictures of the saints, of Mary and Jesus, were simply part of the visual furniture of my imagination from the beginning. So what does that do? Until someone comes along and tells you otherwise, you believe in a world where saints, stars, and planets all happily coexist.

"Which," he was quick to add, "they have long done in places outside my childhood home. . . . There have been plenty of astronomer-priests, from Father Giuseppe Piazzi, who discovered the first asteroid, to Father Angelo Secchi, who developed the first system of classifying stars according to their spectra—that is, the wavelengths of the light they give off. The Vatican has an observatory, and they also maintain a modern research facility here in the States, on Mount Graham in Arizona."

After grade school Bernie attended the Latin School of Indianapolis, an institution dedicated to preparing its students—all boys—for seminary.

"I was very lucky," he told me. "You can't accuse the Catholics of being slouches when it comes to teaching science. The education I got in Algebra, Biology, and Physics—not to mention the classes in the humanities—at that school was on par with what I would have gotten had my parents had the money to send me to some pricey East Coast prep school. Of course, there were also courses in Latin, Rhetoric . . . that kind of thing. Basically, I received a stunningly rounded education, all due to the fact that I was on track to become a priest."

"But then you changed your mind," I pointed out.

"You might say I let the Church down by jumping ship and becoming a scientist in secular institutions," Bernie said. "But in another way, I feel I've done the Church a better service by going out into the world. Because fundamentally that's my whole message. Sure, there are a million discussions—or arguments—that 'science' and 'religion' can have with each other. But beyond, and beneath, all those arguments, there is, I believe, a secret harmony. It's that harmony that I've been focused on, especially in my previous book, *The Purpose-Guided Universe.*"

After graduating from the Latin School at the top of his class, Bernie attended—for a year—a college seminary run by the Benedictine monks of the Saint Meinrad Archabbey in southern Indiana. "It was a place straight out of the Middle Ages," Bernie told me. "The monks in their robes, the early-morning prayers and Gregorian chants. I loved it, in a way. But at the same time, it only took a day or so for me to realize I didn't really belong there. On one level, you could say I left for the most popular reason people leave the priesthood: human weakness. The plain fact was that like most young men my age, I was eager to investigate two lines of study not on the bill at the monastery: beer and girls . . . with emphasis on the latter. But ultimately it was science that lured me away from the monastic life of Saint Meinrad."

For while physics and Gregorian chants could be made to survive side by side at the Latin School of Indianapolis, in the monastery science faded into the background. And for Bernie, that was simply not acceptable. So the following year he left the monastery for Indiana University, and majored in Astrophysics.

He then went on to get his doctorate at the University of Wisconsin in Madison, one of the top schools in the field. He was an excellent student, and when he left school it was for a lifetime of employment at the highest-level institutions.

Bernie never abandoned his belief that science and religion were two parts of a single domain.

But throughout all those years, working at places like the Lockheed Martin Solar and Astrophysics Laboratory, the University of California at Berkeley, the University of Colorado, the Max Planck Institute in Garching, Germany, and the Space Research Laboratory in the Netherlands, Bernie never abandoned his belief that science and religion were two parts of a single domain. No matter how much he learned—and discovered—about the sun, about star formation, about the age and nature of the universe, none of it ever pushed God out of the picture.

"In the sciences today," he told me, "the emphasis is always on practical results. You'd be amazed at how little a student of physics today is taught about the deep conundrums that something like the discipline of quantum physics raises."

Quantum physics, which deals with "quanta," or subatomic particles—as we've already mentioned, the smallest "things" in the physical world—is the single most accurate scientific discovery in history. But quantum physics is also the most mysterious, baffling, and downright frustrating, because its appearance made it necessary for physicists to throw most of what they'd thought they knew up to that point in the trash.

"Much of our technology," Bernie told me, "from cell phones to computers to the navigational devices of airplanes, ships, and submarines, relies on quantum science at some level. University of California physicists Bruce Rosenblum and Fred Kuttner suggest in their book *Quantum Enigma* that fully one-third of our economy is based on quantum theory. Without it, the technological world we take so for granted would grind to a very speedy halt."

Yet from a commonsense perspective—that is, the perspective we see the world from in day-to-day life—quantum physics makes no sense. We can, and do, use it to our great advantage, but crazily enough, we cannot yet explain how it works. It's like a magic machine, allowing us to accomplish all sorts of previously undreamed-of tasks, but with a hood that we simply can't get open to see what makes it run.

I asked Bernie for some examples of these quantum physics conundrums that physicists are still struggling with.

"Well, let's see," he said. "How is it possible for a subatomic (that is, smaller than an atom) particle to carry out instructions coming from the future? From our point of view, this goes against all common sense; how can objects do that? Yet you can perform an experiment involving subatomic particles, and the results of that experiment will depend on how you choose to measure those results *after* the experiment is done. This means that the results of the experiment will retroactively change, depending on how we choose to examine those results."

"So," I said, "it seems important to understand that what you're talking about here is plain facts, not some kind of mental sleight of hand. This is for real . . . right?"

"Yes," said Bernie. "This isn't some semantic trick, some 'way of talking' that makes it appear as if a particle can alter its behavior depending on how we choose to measure it retroactively. *It really happens.* Here," said Bernie, "is another example: How is it possible for a subatomic particle to be in two places at once? A 2003 issue of *Physics News* from the American Institute of Physics carried the headline: '3600 Atoms in Two Places at Once.' Just as linear time is essentially an illusion that we experience but which does not apply if we train our eyes upon the subatomic world, the same goes for an object's existence in physical space. At our level of experience—in the world you and I see and understand—an object is either in one place or another, but not both places at once. But at the subatomic level, objects do not exist in this static, clunky mode. Objects exist in probability fields, which means it is quite easy for a photon, say, to be both 'here' and 'there' at one and the same time.

"This is hard—make that impossible—to envision, because

our imagination is tailored to work at our level of existence. But if you go down small enough, you find a world where nothing acts like we're used to it acting. This isn't, again, an 'illusion.' It's a simple result of the fact that our ordinary ways of understanding are very limited. We simply aren't built to live at that level. But thanks to mathematics and technology, we can enter that world and experience it at one remove, as it were. And what we find, when we do that, is a world that shows us that our ordinary level of perception is an extraordinarily limited one."

I imagined there were scores of physicists out there attempting not just to make sense of these apparent contradictions of the quantum world, but to fathom their religious and philosophical implications. But from Bernie I learned otherwise.

"Sure, there are writers doing that. But there aren't that many serious physicists doing it. At the higher levels of study, and even at the undergraduate level," he told me, "your focus is on practical results, and that only intensifies when you leave school behind and enter professional life. The emphasis is on getting stuff done, and done fast. If some aspect of research doesn't hold some promise for being concretely useful, it doesn't receive funding. So young physicists are not encouraged to spend their time pondering the philosophical implications of the discoveries science has made, and keeps making, in the subatomic realm. If it's not likely to yield profitable results, why bother?

"But," Bernie continued, "I simply didn't see it that way. Getting the practical stuff done was fine, but what I was after was a deeper knowledge. I was happy to do the jobs assigned to me, and I was delighted that my work was good enough to get me hired at places like Lockheed Martin, and to work on and even lead NASA research projects. But neither Lockheed Martin nor NASA are particularly interested in the philosophical or theological implications of physics or astronomy.

"While I was at Lockheed, I produced a very sophisticated star catalog because the CIA needed an ultra-accurate star map to use as a reference for situating their spy satellites. Was I interested in spying? Absolutely not. But I figured: Countries are going to spy on one another. In fact, that is not necessarily a bad thing. Having rivals know each other's capabilities is a good way to keep the peace. If I can help America do a better job of watching what the Russians are up to, well, I don't see anything wrong with that. They were certainly doing the same with us.

"But I personally wasn't there to learn what the Russians were up to. I was there to learn about the universe. I often felt like a university professor when I was doing my NASA-sponsored research . . . except that I did not have any teaching duties. There was also a pretty close relationship between the Lockheed research labs in Palo Alto and Stanford University, just a few blocks away. I considered myself very lucky. The way this generally worked was that NASA would issue a call for proposals. These could range from, say, twenty-five thousand dollars for a small scientific investigation, to major instrument development projects, like the Hubble Space Telescope, approaching a billion dollars or more. If you had a favorite research project that meshed well with the capabilities of a NASA mission, you would write up a request for observing time on that satellite (that is, time to get behind the wheel, as it were, and use the viewpoint provided by the satellite to do exploring of one's own from down here on earth), along with a research justification and a plan for analyzing the data and interpreting the science. A panel of experts would convene to review and rank the proposals. Needless to say, competition was very stiff. One of my favorite research topics was the detection of flares in the ultraviolet and X-ray regions of the spectrum, from stars that are smaller and cooler than the sun. These types of emissions can only be observed from space. It was quite a thrill when my proposal to catch an X-ray flare occurring on Proxima Centauri succeeded using one of the orbiting NASA observatories."

A lot of Bernie's work involved studying the star that we know vastly more about than any other: our sun.

"Our sun formed about 4.6 billion years ago and is about halfway through its hydrogen burning phase. So it's a lightbulb that's about half used up. It's a single star, which is a very great bit of fortune for us because if it had a twin, as many stars do, that would mess up the extreme stability of the orbits of its planets. And we're lucky that the planets move around our sun in orbits that are very close to circular. Sometimes planets circle stars following a more elliptical trajectory, meaning that at certain points they get much closer to their star and at other times much further away. If we had that situation, the earth would alternate between seasons of unimaginable cold and blazing heat. Stability is what you want if you are looking for life, and extreme stability is exactly what we have on earth, thanks to the size and nature of the sun, our distance from it, and the regularity of the distance at which we orbit it.

"The sun is also a much livelier place than people might think," Bernie continued. "We look at it from our perspective and it appears much the same from day to day. But up there, both at the sun's surface and deep within it, it's a different matter. Solar flares, sun spots . . . these things all affect us here on earth in subtle (and sometimes not so subtle) ways. The sun doesn't, obviously, hold physical life. And yet . . . it is an extremely lively place, and of course it's completely responsible for earth being the life-filled place it is. When I consider the sun, I see a source of tremendous mystery and romance. Everything the earth is, and everything you and I are, comes courtesy of the sun. It's beyond me how anyone can look at it with even a trace of boredom."

It occurred to me that for Bernie, the sun was a little like what wolves, sharks, the ocean, and thunderstorms were to me: the place where the world we know overlaps with something beyond that world. I told Bernie about the poet William Blake's famous statement that when an ordinary person looks at the sun, he or she sees an ordinary disk about the size of a ha'penny—a British coin that was in common use in Blake's time. But when Blake looked at the sun, he saw a crowd of angels singing, "Holy, holy, holy is the Lord."

"That's it," said Bernie. "Well, the spirit of it at least. Angels may be up there, but I've never seen them through a telescope."

Bernie, though in a very different way, had been up to what I'd been up to. He'd been going about his business, but all the time he'd had his eye on a figure at the edge of the set: a figure not mentioned in the script, who was in charge of it all.

Immersing myself in a book that tackled such large questions, being the layman to Bernie, the expert, could, I felt, only do me good. No matter how close I got to an answer, the very trying would nourish me.

On our next phone call, I told Bernie that not only was I up for doing a book with him, I even had a title for it.

Of course, I knew what I was getting into with that title. I had discovered that writing books about spiritual subjects with the catchphrase "proof" in the title got on a lot of people's nerves. Eben Alexander, after his rise to fame with *Proof of Heaven*, was subjected to blistering attacks from people both in and out of the scientific community, bemoaning the fact that today, when the existence of a spiritual world had been resoundingly disproved, a Harvard neurosurgeon would have the audacity to produce a book with the words "heaven" and "proof" in the same title. *Proof of Heaven*, the late Oliver Sacks had complained in one review, was not just unscientific, it was anti-scientific.

Voices closer to home agreed. "What's the next one going to be about," a friend of mine had asked recently. *"Proof of the Easter Bunny?"*

I knew, of course, that the notion of a short book claiming to *prove* God's existence was problematic in other ways as well. Philosophers had been trying to prove the existence of God since the days of the ancient Greeks. Scientific proof and religious faith, it was generally agreed, were two different things entirely, and combining them would only serve to further highlight their differences. Suddenly I was going to come along and prove this tried-and-true sentiment wrong?

> *Philosophers had been trying to prove the existence of God since the days of the ancient Greeks. Scientific proof and religious faith, it was generally agreed, were two different things entirely, and combining them would only serve to further highlight their differences.*

I decided I'd see what Bernie thought of the title. After all, he was a serious scientist who'd already told me how much he disapproved of the flaky, irresponsible books about the overlap of science and religion that flooded bookshelves today. He might be outraged at the idea.

He wasn't. "That sounds great," he told me cheerfully when I floated the title to him next time we were on the phone.

Wow, I thought. *That was simple.*

I decided to press Bernie a little more about where he stood on this God business. Did he really and truly *know* God existed?

No, Bernie told me. No scientist worth his salt "knew" anything. The minute you started walking around thinking you knew something, you stopped being a scientist and started being a dogmatist.

"Real scientists," he told me, "don't issue decrees. They are much more likely to say things like 'we think so,' or 'we're not sure.'"

Bernie, I soon discovered, said things like this all the time. Yet when I asked him for a solid number—that is, how sure, percentage-wise, was he that God existed?—he was happy to oblige.

"Ninety-nine percent," he said. "If you're a scientist, nothing's one hundred."

That sounded like a pretty good number to me.

That night, I went up to Colleen's and my bedroom. Getting into bed, I looked at the three koi swimming around in the thirty-gallon tank over on my side of the bed. Koi are carp. They come from Japan and are essentially goldfish, only they're bigger, tougher, and—to my mind—more personable than goldfish, which have always struck me as having a kind of dead, dumb, vacant look.

Koi are likable, but they grow fast—way faster than the man at the fish store who'd sold me my first batch of them had gotten around to telling me they did. Consequently, when I went to bed at night and stared at the koi staring back at me, I'd inevitably feel conflicted. Had one or two of them grown too big for the tank? Was it time for me to take the sad (because I always got attached to them) but necessary step of transferring them from our tank to a friend's pond, where they could swim wild and free and live more fun, if more dangerous (there were no herons or snapping turtles in my aquarium), lives?

"You're projecting," Colleen would sometimes say when I would bring up this issue of whether this or that fish was getting too big for the tank. "You just wish your *own* tank was bigger."

Who doesn't? I'd think when she would tell me this.

Lying there in the semidark of the bedroom, listening to the aquarium's bubble machine toil away, I thought about where things stood with my new project.

Bernie was a scientist: one with good standing in the scientific community. He was also a scientist who believed that God was not a fiction. Acknowledging God's reality was, Bernie felt, central to the human project. Without God, Bernie felt, we were all in trouble.

God was, in Bernie's mind, the sole and supreme reality in the universe, upholding every micron of it at every second. Deprived of God, we could not exist. But . . . we could be deprived of the *knowledge* that He exists, and that was just about as bad.

I believed in God. There was little question for me, personally, that He existed. But did I believe in him *enough?* And was there, perhaps, some new strategy in this belief that Bernie's knowledge could give me?

> *God was, in Bernie's mind, the sole and supreme reality in the universe, upholding every micron of it at every second. But . . . we could be deprived of the knowledge that He exists, and that was just about as bad.*

It occurred to me that if I were to jump with both feet into this project and work to understand what Bernie was saying in as deep a way as I could, my understanding of God, and of the world, might change. A question that had always been at the forefront of my mind, yet out of sight as well, might find a new, and different, and stronger, answer than I had thus far been able to provide.

The aquarium that I lived in might grow a little bigger.

Bernie and I put a proposal together and I submitted it to Howard Books, the publisher of *Proof of Angels*. I showed it to Colleen, and she had only one quibble.

"Just promise me," she said, "that you won't agree to some crazy deadline."

Due to my habit of immediately agreeing to the first deadline date a publisher suggested, I was, when writing a book, in a pretty much constant state of panic. I took a certain sort of pride in being able to produce books not only quickly, but absurdly quickly. In asking that I this time not say "sure" to the first date my publisher suggested, Colleen was attempting to fend off the crash-and-burn phase that was becoming a regular (and unnecessary) stopping point in my book-writing process. Added to this was the fact that I was always writing books in which I almost instantly found myself in over my head. For me, writing a book was like falling through the air, trying to grab as much information as necessary and figure out how things all fit together before I hit the ground.

Truth be told, I kind of liked it that way, even if no one living with me during the process did.

On top of all this, there was the inevitable problem of doing sufficient research in a limited time. Most of the half-dozen books I'd written so far had been produced with the constant anxiety that I was writing about things too deep, too complex, and too fugitive for my abilities. In a way, this was part of the fun—though "fun" wasn't usually the first word that would occur to me each morning when I sat down at my computer. Somewhere about halfway through the writing of whatever book I was working on, the pressure would overwhelm me, and for several weeks the house would become a combination of a mental ward and Mission Control during the *Challenger* crash.

Far from being an exception, this next book showed all the signs of being the clearest demonstration of this habit yet. There had been other dramas in the house that year, and Colleen explained that she just wasn't ready for another book implosion.

"Tell them," she said, "you need a year. They'll understand. There's no reason you need to write what is obviously going to be a challenging book in just six months."

"Okay," I said, "I will."

That was in early May. Two weeks later, I signed a contract promising to have a full manuscript by November 1.

PART II

California

CHAPTER 4

Cortex Troubles

IT WAS AT around this point in the course of Bernie's and my initial talks on the phone that Colleen's and my falling-out occurred, and I suddenly found myself alone in that hotel on the outskirts of town.

Heartsickness is a good state in which to go searching for proof of God's existence, for the simple reason that it drives one to appreciate how painful absence of any kind is. Split up with your wife in middle age, and two words, "absence" and "meaninglessness," swiftly turn from abstractions to harsh, jagged-edged realities.

Marriage is supposed to turn your life into a story. A *happily-ever-after* story. I had just turned fifty-four, and had awakened to discover my life held no narrative . . . no real point, perhaps, at all. It was, to paraphrase Shakespeare, a tale full of sound enough, and fury enough, but signifying nothing, and featuring, as its protagonist, an idiot. The line from that Little Feat song—*Do they really exist at all?*—repeated again and again in my head, with no answer forthcoming.

Heartsickness is a good state in which to go searching for proof of God's existence, for the simple reason that it drives one to appreciate how painful absence of any kind is.

At no point in my life, it seemed to me, had I felt the need for a sense of purpose—within myself and the universe at large—as I did now.

As I sat day after miserable day in the Time Hotel, staring at those skulls on the floor and those tombstones just outside the window, I knew I needed to set about finding that purpose. Bernie, I felt, had an original message, and it was one that many people could benefit from hearing. Too many people had been told for too long that "science" and "materialism" (the belief that immediate physical reality—that is, everything we can physically see and touch—is the only thing there is) were the same thing. Bernie knew they weren't, and—this was the important part—he knew *why* they weren't.

Far too many people had been told by far too many scientists that God was nothing more than a security blanket for people not brave and clearheaded enough to live in the purpose-free universe scientists had been presenting to the public. Bernie, on the other hand, seemed to be a scientist who could talk about God without either dismissing Him or shrinking Him down to the point where, if he existed at all, he was simply another cog in the materialistic machine.

I had, in short, a great project in front of me.

Except for one thing. I was paralyzed because I was so depressed.

An old college friend in California who studies mammals for a living told me on the phone one day that it wasn't surprising I was making zero progress on my book since leaving my house.

"Heavy emotional situations play all kinds of games with your neocortex," she said.

I knew she had a point. The neocortex is the portion of the brain that deals both with logical and analytic functions and with the emotions.

"Obviously you're not getting anything done, because you're too upset. The same triggers in your brain are being activated as would be if you were hiding in a cave thirty thousand years ago with a saber-toothed tiger prowling around outside."

"Well," I said, "things aren't quite *that* bad."

"I know they're not that bad," she said, "but your brain is acting as if they were. The neocortex treats heavy emotional situations in the same way it treats life-and-death ones. That's just how it works. We may live in the modern world, but emotionally we're still in the Stone Age."

I was waiting for her to say, *Especially men*, but she left it at that.

On some level, this bit of insight from my friend in California made me feel better. But not a whole lot better. The depression caused by my separation and the anxiety about my book were mingling in my head like two storm systems. The result was that I continued to waste day after day in that hotel, doing nothing, and not knowing what to do about it.

But after just under a month—and a little over three thousand dollars on my credit card—I started to pull myself together. I asked a friend in LA if I might come out and stay in her guest house for a week or so.

"Sure," she said. "You can go up and visit your astrophysicist friend and then come back down here to do some writing."

The more I thought about it, the more flying out to California made sense. Bernie, worried about what had become of our phone sessions, emailed to find out what the deal was. I explained my situation. He wrote back that I should come out right away.

"Marsha and I," he said, "are both on our third marriages, so we're very sympathetic to your situation. And our son Taylor's room is empty. There's also an empty room next to it you can use as an office, and a guest bathroom too. You're welcome to stay for as long as you want."

I'd known the book would be much better if I actually went out to California and talked to Bernie in person, got an idea of what sort of person he was in three dimensions, saw what his house looked like, met Marsha, and so forth. After all, this was what real, professional-type nonfiction writers did.

But I was a hopeless homebody. I hated travel, and had done my work on both *Proof of Heaven* and *Proof of Angels* without ever setting eyes on Eben or Tyler.

Now, however, I had no excuse for staying where I was.

I got a ticket for Los Angeles, figuring I would stay with my LA friend for a while, then drive up to Bernie's house in Silicon Valley and conduct more interviews with him, as my friend had suggested. I had not been back in my house since my wife's and my falling-out, and I arrived out in California with few possessions. One morning, I walked a few blocks from my friend's house to Deus Ex Machina, an ultra-trendy-looking Australian coffeehouse and clothing/accessories store that had caught my eye because of its unusual name, and picked up a flashy, somewhat oversized key chain that said, simply, *Deus*—"God" in Latin. On it I put the key to my rental car—the only key I had.

When I got back to my friend's house, I showed her the key ring and told her how oddly comforting it was to have it in my pocket, even though there was only one key on it.

My friend rummaged in a drawer. "Here," she said. "It's a key to this house."

I put the key on the chain.

"Wow," I said. "This is so great. It's like having a little . . ."

I couldn't think of the word.

"Dignity," my friend said.

She was right. Not only in terms of the universe, but in the small details of one's life, a person needed to feel like he or she *came* from somewhere. Rootlessness took away one's sense of self, and hence one's self-respect.

> *The scientific questions I was going to be asking Bernie were questions directed not from my brain (though of course my neocortex would play some part in the proceedings) but from my heart, and the more I thought about it, the more right this seemed.*

Another day during that same weeklong stay at my friend's, wandering around in a big antiques emporium near her house, I noticed, behind some costume jewelry and various other uninteresting junk, what looked like a pair of cat's ears carved from stone. I asked one of the people working at the store to open the case, and discovered that the ears belonged to a *maneki-neko,* or Japanese Lucky Cat. Lucky Cats are those friendly, plastic, usually white cat figurines that the proprietors of Asian shops and restaurants place in their front windows to draw in customers and bestow good luck. I knew that though they were typically

68

made of plastic these days, Lucky Cats were originally—like this one—made of stone, and this one was probably a century or so old. I bought the cat, hoping that its benevolent solidness would be a further anchor for me. And in fact, in much the way that that Little Feat song had stuck with me during the first segment of my adventure, that Lucky Cat and key ring stuck with me as durable symbols of this next one.

The scientific questions I was going to be asking Bernie were questions directed not from my brain (though of course my neocortex would play some part in the proceedings) but from my heart, and the more I thought about it, the more right this seemed.

I had no illusions about writing a better book than the countless other ones that were already out there talking about the relationship of religion and science. But I did know I now had one very important thing going for me: desperation.

I was genuinely depressed, not only about my own sad state, but at the sorry state of the universe in general. If, during the long-distance phone calls I'd already had with Bernie, I had asked him questions with enthusiasm and genuine interest, I would now ask them with a new ingredient added: the keen desire to hear something that would cheer me up. I was fifty-four, my marriage was preparing to turn out to be a sad fiasco, and just six years down the line was a number that I had always seen as the end of life, or at least the genuinely vital part of it: sixty.

My father had dreaded the approach of his sixtieth birthday, and here as in many other areas, it seemed I was following him. If I was going to ask Bernie more questions about God, I knew that I'd be asking them with a kind of semi-pathetic earnestness that could, I thought, prove useful. Books written in a state of desperation often had an edge on books written from a position of comfort and ease. I might have been writing a book in a crowded field, but at least I could bank on being much unhappier than the writers of most of those other books had been when they'd written theirs.

> *What I was after was saving information.*
> *The kind that could, if absorbed and*
> *truly understood, help a person to better*
> *navigate life and its struggles.*

T. S. Eliot, my favorite poet, wrote in his "Four Quartets" that old men should be explorers. In younger years, this line had sounded sort of silly, but the older I got, the less silly it seemed, and the more it sounded like an ideal. One worth, perhaps, living up to.

Another realization followed from all this, and that was that I needed to keep what I was getting from Bernie not only clear, clean, and sharply defined, but *emotionally useful*. The information I was looking for was not "interesting" information, though I figured Bernie would be able to dish plenty of that. What I was after was *saving* information. The kind that could, if absorbed and truly understood, help a person to better navigate life and its struggles.

All kinds of bona fide scientists were telling people that "God" was a word whose shelf life had expired. I needed to mine Bernie's brain not for some sweeping survey of modern science, but a few key facts.

In fact, I realized, the book would itself have to be a kind of key ring. It needed to present a small set of ideas that were both easy to grasp and genuinely useful: ideas that could act as keys to unlock the door to a universe that wasn't pointless and dead but rich with hope and life and meaning.

I now just needed to find out, with Bernie's help, what those keys were to be.

CHAPTER 5

Computer Land

DRIVING ON HIGHWAY 5 up the California corridor to Redwood City, the Silicon Valley town Bernie and Marsha lived in, I tried to picture the house I was heading to. I associated Silicon Valley with Internet start-ups, with Google and Yahoo!, with the HBO series of the same name . . . all the usual stuff. I imagined a bland, generic place but, most likely, a comfortable one.

For what seemed like the millionth time, I assessed my situation: Here I was, with no family to speak of, with *nothing* to speak of, driving up to a house I'd never been to before, to spend time with a man I'd never met, in order to prove the existence of God. The absurdity of it all reminded me of the famous, and disastrously depressing, quote of physicist Steven Weinberg: "The more the universe seems comprehensible, the more it also seems pointless." For a few fleeting moments during that drive up Highway 5, I wondered if Weinberg might just have been right after all.

After some five hours, I pulled off of the 5 and made my way through a landscape of strawberry and artichoke fields, past vegetable stands with big white homemade signs featuring hand-painted pictures of strawberries and corn reminiscent of a John Steinbeck novel. Then I got onto the 101, and the landscape around me slowly lost its sparse, hilly openness and filled up with low, anonymous-looking buildings that I imagined were full of people typing code and holding meetings about global market reach.

By early evening, when I hit Bernie's exit just north of Palo Alto, I was a nervous wreck. Though I was simply visiting a comfortable house in a bland but benign suburb of San Francisco, my emotion-scrambled neocortex was making me feel like I was jumping out of a plane behind enemy lines. All that old rubbery-ness I'd had in my twenties, when I happily went anywhere, anytime, with no money or plans, was gone. My mental/emotional brake pads, I noted sadly, were worn down to the metal. If only I was back in what I'd thought was my basement, getting all this done on the phone and enduring one of those smaller, safer, and entirely more manageable book-writing breakdowns that I usually had, instead of this grimly major one.

My iPhone led me to Bernie's street with its usual unnerving efficiency, and the neighborhood proved to be pretty much what

I'd expected: large houses, most with two-, some with three-, car garages. In front of some of these, impeccably maintained cars from the sixties and early seventies were parked next to Mercedes and BMWs.

Bernie and Marsha both came out to greet me. Marsha was all smiles and warmth, while Bernie, wearing the baggy track-suit that turned out to be his standard around-the-house out-fit, was more shy and businesslike. Marsha was a tall, attractive blond, with a sixties "flip" hairstyle. There was something about her that suggested a former hippie who had since made herself at home in suburbia. The kind of woman who dresses crisply and conventionally, but wears necklaces with beads that are just a little big and a little bright.

I noticed that Bernie had a pronounced limp. No, it wasn't a limp exactly. Bernie took small, delicate steps, almost like a horse trotting very carefully.

"Bernie's got Parkinson's," Marsha said, matter-of-factly but just ever so slightly out of Bernie's earshot, as we headed into the house behind him. "He probably didn't tell you, did he?"

"No, he didn't," I said. I knew several people with Parkin-son's, and was familiar with what a tough disease it was. I knew, also, that the disease attacked not only the body but the brain. It thus put the person suffering from it constantly on guard, wondering if a momentarily forgotten name or phone number was just ordinary forgetfulness, or the first fingerholds of some-thing larger and darker. I thought of what it must be like to be someone like Bernie, with a stunning command of mathematics, physics, and who knew what else, having to cope with not knowing whether the vast store of facts at his disposal would be there the next time he reached for it.

Marsha directed me down a hall hung with pictures, most of which looked to be a decade or so old, of her and Bernie on various vacations. Most were ski trips, with the two of them, skis lined up side by side, poles in hand, smiling at the camera while standing atop this or that mountain in Europe or the American West.

"Here's Taylor's room," Marsha said, showing me a disconcertingly tight space taken up almost completely by a bed, a piano stacked with back issues of the *Journal of Scientific Exploration*, the magazine Bernie and Marsha had edited for ten years, and a low chest of drawers piled high with videos, both DVDs and VHS cassettes.

Looking closer, I saw that they all seemed to feature the Three Stooges. *A Plumbing We Will Go* read the DVD box on top of one stack, showing the Stooge Curly, dressed in plumber's garb, wrestling with a comically twisted water pipe.

I knew that—inexplicably, to my mind—Bernie had a soft spot for the Stooges. In *The Purpose-Guided Universe*, there is a long section in which Moe, Larry, and Curly demonstrate the paradoxes of Heisenberg's Uncertainty Principle using pennies that are either sliced in half or lengthwise. Curly mails a penny to Moe, who is astonished to find that the penny in the envelope is sliced either vertically or lengthwise depending on his expectations of how it will be sliced, just as subatomic particles are able to anticipate how experimenters will choose to measure them, before the experimenters themselves have decided on how they will do so. There are a lot of "nyuk-nyuks" and "soitenlys" in the section, and Bernie was especially proud of it—so much so that, back during our phone conversations from my basement, he'd said, "I hope we can get that Stooges segment into the book. I worked hard to make the all-important measurement problem in quantum mechanics understandable with a little help from Larry, Moe, and Curly."

"Sure," I'd answered vaguely, picturing, perhaps, an appendix where we could stow the thing. Suddenly, looking at all those Stooge films, it came to me: No wonder he didn't mind that in our first conversations I had come across as something of an idiot in matters of physics. He *liked* idiots.

Bernie and Marsha had had dinner already, so I said I'd go out to the mall I'd passed just before their turnoff and find something quick to eat there. I found a Mexican place, ordered a burrito, and felt just about as lonely and isolated as I figured it was possible to feel. I stared at the key ring on the table in front of me. It now had three keys on it—the one to the house of my friend in LA, my rental car key, and a key to Bernie and Marsha's. And, on the same ring with the keys, that single word in metal and bright red enamel: *Deus.*

And it occurred to me, again, what I was going to do—or what I was going to try to do, in these days with Bernie.

My friend down in LA had been right. That key ring, with its simple solidity, its simple *there*-ness, had anchored me somehow. If there was anything in today's world that people needed, I thought, it was a kind of mental key ring: an easy-to-carry set of core truths that, if used correctly, could open doors to genuine possibility and hope about our true place and stature in the universe. If Bernie was convinced God existed, and he had knowledge that could back up his statements so that they couldn't be quashed by all those atheist/materialist science writers (and book reviewers) out there, then I would do my best to convey his insights in a way that could reach people—as many people as possible—who might not otherwise encounter these ideas, and who might genuinely be helped by them.

All I needed to do now was talk to Bernie some more, and get settled on what, exactly, those key truths were going to be.

Piece of cake.

CHAPTER 6

The Field

Bernie's and my first person-to-person interview took place in his office the following morning. Marsha was already busy. She is a classically trained singer and music teacher, and teaches up to six students a day in voice, piano, or guitar, most of them kids. We could hear her first student uncertainly practicing his scales upstairs as we began our talk.

The space was about what one would expect from a semiretired astrophysicist: papers and books stacked all over, a desk with a big computer monitor on it, and a couple of rolling chairs. I sat in one, Bernie sat in the other; I turned on the voice memo function on my iPhone, and we got down to business.

I decided that if I was going to explain Bernie to the world at large, I needed to start with the startling fact that he wasn't positive that the Higgs Boson, or so-called "God Particle," which had received such a tremendous amount of press just a few years previously, was necessarily the big deal it was supposed to be. During our sessions over the next few days, Bernie stated repeatedly that he was not denying the Higgs Particle. "I guess you could say I'm just keeping a healthy skepticism because of the work that Rueda, Puthoff, and I did on the question of inertia, and published, back in the 1990s."

From my previous research I knew there was a story behind this inertia stuff, but to get things off to an easy start, I decided to cover some basic intro questions.

"Why did you write your first book, *The God Theory*?"

"Well, basically," Bernie said, "when I was twenty-seven, my first marriage broke up."

"How come?"

"Oh, the usual reason for first marriages breaking up. We were too young."

The inevitable depression and soul-searching brought on by the divorce had gotten Bernie thinking.

"It seemed to me that as an astrophysicist with an interest in spiritual matters, maybe I was in a position to share some ideas about how these two supposedly warring ways of thinking could actually live together under one roof. I started doing some reading, but then I got offered a job at an observatory in Holland. Between moving to a new country and tackling the new job, my spare time went down to zero. So I put the project on the shelf."

It stayed there a long time. One job followed another, and over the next few decades Bernie had lengthy stints at some of the world's major centers of physics and astronomy. But twenty-seven years after shelving that initial project on science and spirituality, Bernie found himself, at last, with time to devote to a question which, in all those intervening years, he'd never lost his interest in. With the plethora of anti-God books that started coming out in the early years of the new millennium, he was more convinced than ever that the world needed to hear from serious scientists who were on God's side. Now that he was semi-retired (he was a part-time faculty member at Foothill College tutoring in Math and Astronomy), he had the time to revisit the big questions.

The results of that conviction, so far, had been his two books and a number of speaking engagements at conferences and universities around the country and beyond. In all of these, he'd made the case that science and religion were not enemies but two aspects of a single truth.

For obvious reasons, I found it interesting that Bernie's first inkling that he wanted to take a stab at helping to unify science and religion had come in the wake of his first divorce. Because if there's one thing divorces are, it's disorienting. One's footing in the world is tested—and, usually, found wanting. That lack of orientation creates a realization that, even when we are at our happiest and most secure, few of us in the modern world feel genuinely on course in the world we live in, for the very good reason that we don't know what that course is, or even *if* it is.

"I wanted," Bernie told me, "to write something that would make it possible for people with faith in God and a trust in science to be able to say: 'Well, there's more to the world than I'm being taught, and I'm not going to let any supposed conflicts between these two areas of my life stand in the way of finding out what's real.'"

"Marriages," I said, "are built on trust. You place your complete trust in your partner, and they in turn place their complete trust in you—at least ideally. When the trust that's supposed to be at work in a marriage breaks up, it produces—at least in some people—a question about the larger implications of trust, and specifically, whether there is anything in this world that we truly *can* place our trust in, unconditionally. Conventional science gives us nothing in this department, except maybe for the scientific method (the process of observation, experimentation, and drawing conclusions from the results of that experimentation that has given us so much of our knowledge of the physical world). But the scientific method," I added, "isn't much help on a lonely Saturday night."

"I believe," said Bernie, "that it's possible to have a trust in both science *and* in spirituality, and to live a life that's based upon that dual trust. It's pretty obvious that religion isn't going away, even though for a long time a lot of people thought it was going to. But if science and spirituality remain at odds, or at least *appear* to be at odds, that creates a problem. That business about them being unrelated, with no overlap between them whatsoever—I think that's nonsense."

Bernie was here referring to paleontologist Stephen Jay Gould's idea, put forward in the nineties, of *non-overlapping magisteria*. The idea at the bottom of this grand-sounding term was that science dealt with facts, and religion dealt with values.

"A man cannot serve two masters," I said, quoting from Matthew's gospel.

> *It's pretty obvious that religion isn't going away, even though for a long time a lot of people thought it was going to. But if science and spirituality remain at odds, or at least appear to be at odds, that creates a problem.*

"I believe that's really true," Bernie said, perhaps a bit surprised to hear me quoting from the Bible. "I think a lot of people would be genuinely surprised how many unsolved scientific problems there currently are in which the best explanation is simply: 'God did it.' The world needs to learn a new set of basic facts about the universe we live in. Facts that are established, that bring an incredible new world into focus, but that, at the moment, too few people know about."

In other words, I thought, a *ring with some keys on it.*

"Okay," I said, "let's get on to the Higgs Boson, the supposed 'God Particle.' Why did the discovery of the Higgs Boson make such a big splash in the popular media? Why were people calling it the 'God Particle' to begin with? I never quite got what it had to do with God, especially since it appeared that its discoverers didn't even believe in God to begin with."

To my surprise, Bernie seemed slightly taken aback by the question.

"Well, I wasn't really expecting to talk about that stuff," he said.

"You weren't expecting to talk about it?" I said. "That seems, well, kind of weird. I mean, here you and Rueda came up with this whole alternate theory to the one that two scientists won the Nobel Prize for just three years ago. Doesn't that seem like something that ought to be in the book?"

"Well," said Bernie, "I guess so. It's just a little beside the point now that the Higgs Particle seems to be in the bag."

"But," I said, "as far as I understand it, you still think Rueda's and your theory of inertia might be correct. If you don't think it stands a chance of being correct, then I agree we ought to ditch it."

"Oh, well, sure," said Bernie, still with a dismissive tone to his voice, "we might be right. You never know."

"Well," I said, feeling like I was explaining something to a fifth-grader, "if you *are* right, that's your clearest chance at scientific immortality. You, um, *are* interested in scientific immortality, aren't you, Bernie?"

"Oh, I guess so," Bernie said, with a tone that translated pretty clearly into: *No, I'm not. I'm interested in something much more important.*

"But yes, okay," Bernie said. "The discovery of the Higgs Boson was a big deal because the Higgs Field is thought to be responsible for the creation of mass, or rather the illusion of mass, in the universe."

"Okay," I said. "So solidity, the feeling of substantiality that I feel in every object I interact with, its hardness, its weight—everything that makes it feel like something that really exists, that's really there—that comes from its mass. I also know that when viewed at a really, really small level, the world has a lot less actual mass in it than we imagine it does. You know, all the usual stuff about how an object—this table, for example—is something like 99.999999 percent empty space. But what you seem to be saying goes beyond even that. You're saying that even the actual, massy, genuinely solid part of this table . . . that's an illusion too."

Mass is, essentially, what gives things their feeling of solidity. A penknife in your pocket feels heavy and hard because of its mass. A giant, immovable boulder is immovable because of its mass. Bang your head against the boulder, and your head will hurt because your skull, and the brain inside it, also possess mass. Without mass, our world would quite simply have nothing in it. In fact, we would *have* no world, for the world is, of course, made up of objects, and without mass, those objects would not be able to exist.

"Basically," I said, "I thought that mass, though it formed a very small part of the world, was something that was just *there.*"

"Not at all," said Bernie. "Mass certainly isn't just 'there.' In fact, as I said, its existence is in itself an illusion. The physical world, as you know, is made up of atoms of different elements, which join together to form molecules. Hydrogen is an atom. Oxygen is an atom. Two hydrogen atoms and an oxygen atom give you a molecule of water, H_2O."

"Atoms, the building blocks of elements, have a nucleus, the thing that's in the middle, like the pit inside a peach, that's made up of neutrons and protons. Protons have a positive charge, like the 'plus' end of a battery, and neutrons have no charge."

"Right," I said, confidently rattling off what I'd learned in Mr. Caiola's Chemistry class back in eleventh grade. "Atoms, the building blocks of elements, have a nucleus, the thing that's in the middle, like the pit inside a peach, that's made up of neutrons and protons. Protons have a positive charge, like the 'plus' end of a battery, and neutrons have no charge. They clump together really tightly, thanks to the strong force, one of the four key forces known to science, a kind of miniature version of gravity that's super-powerful but only works at very, very close distances. It makes the protons and neutrons in an atom bunch really close together. Meanwhile, the atom's electrons, which have a negative charge—like the other end of that battery—swirl around the nucleus of the atom, like planets orbiting the sun. Sort of."

I threw that "sort of" in because I knew that the super-simplified model of the atom that Mr. Caiola had drawn on the blackboard for us, with the protons and neutrons bunched in the middle and the electrons whizzing around way out at the atom's perimeter, had been essentially debunked. Electrons, I knew, didn't "move" in the same way as objects in the ordinary world do. In fact, electrons were so dodgy that it was impossible to establish an electron's exact speed *and* its exact position in space at the same time. You could nail down an electron's speed, or you could (almost) nail down an electron's position, but you could not do both at once. This was because electrons, and other subatomic particles—that is, all the small "things" that are dwarfed even by atoms—don't really exist in one exact place, ever. Electrons, and all other particles, are more accurately described as "particle fields" because, strictly (if illogically) speaking, they never, ever hold totally still. They can't, because they're not really solid objects at all, but something more like tiny knots of energy. The minute you think you've got your finger on one, *ping!* It shoots out, leaving you with nothing.

> *Electrons, and all other particles,*
> *are more accurately described as "particle*
> *fields" because, strictly (if illogically)*
> *speaking, they never, ever hold totally still.*
> *They can't, because they're not really solid*
> *objects at all, but something more like tiny*
> *knots of energy.*

"Yeah," said Bernie. "That's about right. Our universe, or the part of the universe that we can measure, is made up of basically three things: protons, neutrons, and electrons. Compared to protons and neutrons, electrons are super-small. They're actually particles, the smallest units of matter yet discovered. But particles are not only small, they're, as you say, actually not 'things' at all, at least not in the way we are used to thinking. Particles are so small, and exist so close to the borderline between existence and nonexistence, that they are capable of simply vanishing. They can literally disappear."

> *"Our universe, or the part of the universe that we can measure, is made up of basically three things: protons, neutrons, and electrons."*

"Where do they go when they disappear?" I asked.

In classic fashion, Bernie said simply: "We don't know."

CHAPTER 7

"You're Soaking in It."

"**O**KAY," I SAID. "So the universe, or at least the universe that we can measure, is made up of protons, neutrons, and electrons. But protons and neutrons are actually not the solid little BB-type things we see in textbooks, but are themselves made up of particles. And those, it seems, are made of . . . what? Energy, right?"

"Particles are essentially just congealed little knots of energy. Because, of course, energy and matter are, at bottom, the same thing."

"Roger that. Particles are essentially just congealed little knots of energy. Because, of course, energy and matter are, at bottom, the same thing. That's what Einstein discovered, and what he told the world about in his famous theorem $E = mc^2$, where 'c' equals the speed of light, about 670,000,000 miles per hour, or 186,000 miles per second."

"It's funny," I said. "That equation is one that just about everyone knows. Yet to someone not comfortable with mathematics, it is just hopelessly remote. I mean, *why* does the energy contained in a certain unit of matter equal that unit of matter times the speed of light squared?"

"Don't get hung up on the numbers," Bernie said. "That just reflects the system of units we use to measure these things: units that are in essence arbitrary, like your speedometer registering speed in miles per hour in the US but kilometers per hour in Europe. What really matters is that it is possible to change one thing (motion) into another, different thing (energy). What does matter is that the speed of light is the limit, in our universe, for how fast something can go. Neither light nor anything else can go faster. Why does light travel at that speed? The cheap and easy answer—which, I'm afraid, is the one we're going to have to stay with, if you don't want this book to explode into a physics textbook—is because that number is a constant of the world we live in—the world of space-time. It's one of the irreducible givens of the world we find ourselves living in. Why does energy equal matter times the speed of light squared? We are dealing with absolute fundamentals here—the wood and the nails God used to construct our universe. As we will, I think, discover later, there are often no good answers (other than the God one) for why our universe is constructed in such a way that this or that mathematical equation happens to be able to describe it. These are simply the nature and dimensions of the materials with which God built the tabernacle of our universe."

"Okay, fair enough," I said. "But so, to get back to particles—the smallest known objects in our universe. I understand how they are very squirrelly things to deal with, that they don't like to hold still, to be confined in one place at one time. But . . . why don't they come equipped with mass?"

"Because," said Bernie, "as we covered when we talked about the Higgs Field, *nothing in the universe actually possesses mass.* Particles, and hence all the things that are made up of them (that is, everything in the world, including you and me and this desk and those trees outside the window and whatever else you might want to name) only appear to have mass. This means that in order to appear to be solid, to be massy, particles need something to resist their motion."

> *"Nothing in the universe actually possesses mass. Particles, and hence all the things that are made up of them . . . only appear to have mass."*

"You mean, something to rub up against?"

"Sure. Kind of like moving through molasses. Whenever a

particle speeds up, it encounters resistance. But resistance from what? That's the sixty-four-thousand-dollar question. It could be the Higgs Field or it could be something else."

"So," I said, "truth be told, there's nothing solid in the universe at all."

"Well, it depends on how you look at it. But yes, if you are talking about something like a marble or a ball bearing that *seems* solid to us, you could definitely say there's no such thing in the universe. Marbles and ball bearings are swirling clouds of energy, that's all. There's nothing to them."

> *"Marbles and ball bearings are*
> *swirling clouds of energy, that's all.*
> *There's nothing to them."*

"Okay," I said. "But the reason we are able to have the illusion of solidity—the reason I can feel the coins in my pocket, or this chair I'm sitting in, as being solid, as being actually there—that's because of the Higgs Field. The field these particles rub up against that makes them appear to have mass. The Higgs Field is like this universal, invisible 'stuff' that's absolutely everywhere. We can't see it, we can't feel it, but because it's there, when particles move against it, they create a kind of friction, and that rubbing against the field, if you will, gives them the appearance of having mass."

"Right," said Bernie. "That's exactly what the Higgs Field does. It's a kind of super molasses . . . that is, if it really exists."

It looked like I was on my way to getting Bernie to talk some more about his potential discovery after all.

"So you're disputing that those people who found the Higgs Field, and the Higgs Boson, or 'God Particle,' really found what they thought they found."

"That's too strong a statement. They found *something*," Bernie said. "They found what looks, from preliminary analysis, to be a new kind of particle, and might quite possibly *be* the Higgs Particle. Now, the Higgs Particle has been around for a while. It was first hypothesized to exist in papers published in 1964 by six authors, one of whom was a theoretical physicist named Peter Higgs. The existence of the particle would have tied up a number of vexing questions in the physics field, not least of which was the question of what allows apparent mass to exist in our universe. Consequently, physicists have been searching for it ever since."

"So, just to be clear," I said, "we're talking about two things here—the Higgs Particle and the Higgs Field. Why are both so important?"

"Because," said Bernie, "fields and particles are two sides of the same coin. Every particle has a field that it acts in relation to. All particles possess their own fields. So if you have a Higgs Particle, it follows that there's a Higgs Field out there, and that it's this field that has the function of creating virtual mass, and hence virtual matter. Without that particle, and the field that goes along with it, there would be no mass in the universe. So when the Higgs Particle was (apparently) discovered, that meant, to simplify things quite a bit, that the Higgs Field had been discovered too. So it's thought that those scientists discovered the answer to one of the great questions physicists had been trying to answer: What creates the feeling of solidity, of mass, in the world? What gives the world its permanence and stability?"

I had to admit that I still didn't have much of a grasp on what the Higgs Field was. Truth be told, I didn't have a grasp on what *any* kind of field was. I certainly got that fields, whatever they were, were important—were central—if you wanted to get even the most basic understanding of what the material world was and how it worked. But somehow the word "field" itself held me back.

I mean, what is a field?

My mind went back to those koi in my aquarium in Nyack. It seemed like a gamble (I could only take this *physics for boneheads* thing so far), but I decided to take it.

"So look," I said. "It seems to me that if you're going to give me a basic understanding of the kind of universe you live in, which is clearly closer to reality than the one I'm living in, I'm going to have to understand what a field is. But I have to tell you, I don't have the remotest grasp of what a field really is. I can't envision it.

"So let me try something out on you. I have these fish back home. Koi, you know, like goldfish. Every night, when I'd go to bed, I'd stare at those koi, and I'd watch them bump up against the walls of their aquarium, and when we started our talks, and I got into your books, I found myself thinking that fields are kind of like the water those fish were in. They completely lived in that water, yet they were so much in it that they scarcely took notice of it. So . . . for the purposes of this book, can I envision a field as being somewhat like the water in that aquarium? They're invisible, everywhere-present elements that we're totally immersed in, even though we don't notice them, don't experience them, at all?"

> *"They're invisible, everywhere-present elements that we're totally immersed in, even though we don't notice them, don't experience them, at all?"*

Bernie thought for a moment. "Sure, the fish tank analogy works."

"So . . . you're not that surprised that I don't really understand what fields are?"

"Well, no," said Bernie. "Because the fact of the matter is that no one does. In fact, they may very well not exist at all."

"They don't exist *either*? I give up."

"It's like this," said Bernie. "Let's say one particle, or one atom, affects another particle, or atom, and that they're some distance apart—a few feet, say. It doesn't really matter. Let's say there was no physical contact between the two particles or atoms, yet somehow one affected the other. How do you explain this? Science explains it by suggesting *fields*, or invisible forces that are present everywhere, through which matter in one place can affect matter in some other place. The fields are a kind of projection of the properties of the particle, such as the electric charge."

"Well, that's helpful. So there are different kinds of fields in the universe, and we're going to leave it at that, because it sounds like science doesn't have a complete handle on what fields are anyway. But . . . given that there are different kinds of fields in the universe (even though you just told me that fields might not even exist either), is the Higgs Field the only one we need to worry about?"

"Far from it," said Bernie. "In fact, the whole reason that my associates and I took issue with the Higgs Field was because there was this other field, much closer to hand, that we felt would do the job of explaining the existence of mass in our universe much better. That field is called the Zero Point Field. Let's do a quick thought experiment. If you were to take a cubic centimeter of space and suck every last atom of oxygen, nitrogen, and whatever else out of it, so that, atomically and molecularly speaking, there was absolutely nothing left in that cubic centimeter of space, what would you have left?"

"Um. A vacuum?" I ventured.

"Yes," said Bernie, "you *would* have a vacuum, if it were possible for an absolute vacuum to exist in our universe. However, it isn't. Everywhere, at every moment, trillions upon trillions of particles are coming into existence and then disappearing back out of it. They pop into existence, then either crash into each other so that both are instantly annihilated, or they simply pop back out of existence on their own. And they do this so fast— something along the lines of a trillion trillionth a second in any cubic centimeter in the world around you—that they don't exist long enough to have any kind of measurable effect on the world."

> *"One cubic centimeter of empty space in this room has enough energy in it to blow up the universe, or at least a good chunk of it."*

"Okay," I said. "But . . . they're *there*, even if they come into existence and go out of existence so fast that they don't have an effect on the world . . . other than creating inertia."

"Yes," said Bernie. "Though, as the Soviet nuclear physicist Andrei Sakharov proposed, they may also produce gravitation— but that's another story. The gist is this: one cubic centimeter of 'empty space' in this room has enough energy in it to blow up the universe. The Zero Point Field is an invisible but vast sea of energy that moves in and out of existence so fast that it might as well not be there as far as we're concerned. Except that it *is* there. And it's so powerful that if you could harness it, one cubic centimeter of 'empty' space would provide enough energy to solve all of humanity's energy needs for the rest of humankind's time on earth, no matter how long that might be.

> *"If you could harness it, one cubic centimeter of 'empty' space would provide enough energy to solve all of humanity's energy needs for the rest of humankind's time on earth, no matter how long that might be. . . . That fact—and it is a fact—is a potent illustration of just how much we miss of the real world, living, as we do, bound by our five senses and the limitations of our human minds."*

"If nothing else, that fact—and it is a fact that this Zero Point Field does exist—is a potent illustration of just how much we miss of the real world, living, as we do, bound by our five senses and the limitations of our human minds. Mystics—both the many Christian ones and those of other faiths as well—are, I believe, capable of connecting intuitively with aspects of our world that normal people can't. They have had glimpses into that world of energy and fire that is hiding behind this presumably ordinary, presumably humdrum world that science has purported to have explained. But for ordinary people like you and me, the existence of something like the Zero Point Field must be confined to theory. Something, in short, we must take on faith."

"So," I asked, "could somebody harness that energy?"

"Not now, not today," said Bernie. "But someday . . who knows? And not only does the Zero Point Field potentially hold the solution to our energy dilemmas; it may also allow us to harness the force of gravity, so that objects—no matter how heavy—could be moved with no effort at all. The Field also might hold the key to how we might be able to build crafts capable of traveling to other worlds—worlds far too distant, now, for our technology to come even close to getting to. This obviously also raises the question of whether other civilizations have used this technique to get here—something I'm not qualified to comment on beyond simply raising the possibility.

"But of course, this is all just wild guessing. Yet the wild theories of today often become the realities of tomorrow. That's why Arthur C. Clarke used the theory that Rueda, Puthoff, and I came up with in a novel of his—an adaptation of which," he said with apparent amusement, "appeared in this 'scientific journal.'"

Bernie reached behind him to fumble among some papers, and produced, to my surprise, the March 1998 edition of *Playboy*.

On page 76 of the magazine was a story written by Clarke and Stephen Baxter called "The Wire Continuum."

"In the story," Bernie said, "Clarke and Baxter create something called the 'HRP Effect.' The HRP standing for Haisch, Rueda, and Puthoff. Of course, Clarke was writing science fiction, but I was flattered that he thought enough of our theory to build an elaborate, and carefully researched, story around it."

"Wow," I said. "So you're part of an Arthur C. Clarke story in *Playboy*. Looks like that whole scientific immortality challenge has already been met."

"Well," said Bernie, "they call it science *fiction* for a reason. Nonetheless, as people like to say, yesterday's science fiction often becomes tomorrow's scientific fact, and though it's way too premature to think about such possibilities in any but the most theoretical of ways, think of all the feats science performs today that were unthinkable a hundred, or fifty, or even twenty years ago."

"So what does the name 'Zero Point Field' mean?"

"The 'Zero' in 'Zero Point Field' comes from the fact that the field is still present at absolute zero temperature, the coldest temperature possible, when most atomic processes grind to a halt. What that means, in essence, is that the power of the Zero Point Field is so unimaginably great that it transcends temperature itself. All of which is to say that the Zero Point Field is a force that's powerful far, far beyond our capacity to imagine. It makes the power in a nuclear explosion look like firecrackers. It could toast our universe in a microsecond, and yet here we are, right now, existing in the very midst of it."

"*You're soaking in it*," I said, absently.

"What?" said Bernie.

"It's a commercial from the seventies," I said. "For Palmolive dishwashing liquid. There's this woman named Madge. She was, like, a beautician I think. Anyhow, in the commercial, she's doing this woman's fingers, soaking them in this liquid. Madge talks to the woman about how she should use Palmolive dishwashing liquid, because it softens your hands while you do the dishes. Then she says to the lady: 'You know you're soaking in it.' The lady freaks out, and says: 'Dishwashing liquid?' And then Madge says: 'Relax, it's Palmolive.'"

"I never saw it," said Bernie. "Too bad I missed that one, I guess."

"Wow, really? Well," I said, "you probably watched a good deal less TV in the seventies than I did. Anyhow, it just somehow reminded me of the commercial, what you were saying about how we're all immersed in this incredible field of energy right now, but we don't even know it. It also makes me think of the lines 'For in him we live and move and have our being.'"

"What?" Bernie said, perhaps gearing up for another memory of a seventies television commercial.

"You know," I said. "Paul says it in *Acts*. He talks about God as something, or Someone, in whom 'we live, and move, and have our being.' I always liked that, because the words give me this sense of total immersion in God. They make me think about how, like I said, I'm like a fish that doesn't know what water is, because I'm totally immersed in it."

Bernie looked a bit annoyed: "I hope you're not getting all new agey about this. People who have probably never taken a physics course tell me stuff like that: saying the Zero Point Field is God."

He gave me an "I'm checking you out" look, and then continued.

"To acknowledge the reality of the Zero Point Field, and its possible role in creating the illusion of the solid world, is science. To call the Zero Point Field God is simply to take tantalizingly complex and mysterious scientific facts and reduce them to woolly, cool-sounding words that don't tell us anything. God could not *be* the Zero Point Field. God isn't anything *in this universe* we live in. He transcends it, is beyond it, is in no way caught up in its mechanisms. That's standard theology, but it's also the first thing to take into account if you want to risk talking about 'God' and 'science' in the same breath. That's why I get so upset about all these books that talk about the Zero Point Field as if it's this mystical thing, the answer to the big question of where God is and what he's like. Well, God may have made sure that our Universe came with a Zero Point Field but that is a far, far cry from saying that God *is* the Zero Point Field. That's just absurd."

"Sure," I said. "That way of talking about it actually echoes the way Jesus talks in the Gospels. When Jesus talks about the Kingdom, he's highly specific, highly concrete, yet at the same time very careful not to lock his statements down. He's very careful to remind us, at all times, that this is what he is saying the Kingdom is *like*, not what it *is*. He uses all these very concrete metaphors that a peasant from his time would easily be able to understand. The pearl of great price in Matthew, for example:

"'Again, the kingdom of heaven is like unto a merchant man, seeking goodly pearls: Who, when he had found one pearl of great price, went and sold all that he had, and bought it.'

"That pearl is so valuable that the merchant sells everything he has to get it. Is this some ordinary pearl? Obviously not. Does Jesus go into greater detail about what's so special about it? Of course not. But when it comes to saying just what that 'it' is, he's elusive. Or take the parable of the mustard seed from Matthew:

"'The kingdom of heaven is like to a grain of mustard seed, which a man took, and sowed in his field: Which indeed is the least of all seeds: but when it is grown, it is the greatest among herbs, and becometh a tree, so that the birds of the air come and lodge in the branches thereof.'"

"Of course," said Bernie, "he's speaking in metaphors. He doesn't say the kingdom of heaven is a seed, but that it shares qualities with it."

"Right," I said. "But intriguingly, there is a lot of talk of the seemingly small turning out to be exceedingly great. Maybe," I said, half tongue-in-cheek, "if Jesus were alive today, he would say the Kingdom is like the Zero Point Field. It's everywhere, its tiniest point contains more power than we can conceive. Yet, despite the fact that we're immersed in it, that we're soaking in it, as Madge would say, we don't see it.

"God, the fifteenth-century German philosopher and theologian Nicholas of Cusa wrote, is a circle whose center is everywhere, and whose circumference is nowhere. I see a connection here: The field is an everywhere-present but completely invisible and undetectable ocean of light that makes the world feel solid. In doing so, it allows us to have a physical universe, or rather an *apparent* physical universe, to live and move through. Like God, the field lends us our being. Like God it is closer to us than our own jugular vein. Like God it is invisible yet everywhere. No wonder so many new-age writers have been talking it up.

"Yes," Bernie said. "And as I said, that's just the problem. We shouldn't get too fixated on the Zero Point Field, especially as the Higgs Particle may prove to be as mighty a discovery as many people think it is. We need to wait and see. I'll also keep the Zero Point Field inertia model in my back pocket for the time being. The reason I wanted to write this book with you is because in my observation there is more and more evidence forthcoming, *and forthcoming from the realm of twenty-first century science*, that there is some kind of a great intelligence behind the laws of nature. It goes way beyond the Higgs or Zero

Point Field. The evidence of a great creative intelligence ranges from the bizarre behavior of quantum experiments to the evolution of the cosmos. People should know this. This is the kind of knowledge you should take into account when you decide what you truly believe.

"It's amazing, the things we don't know," Bernie said. "It's also amazing what we *do* know, and it's amazing what a help to a lot of people those things could be if they were just told about them . . . which, again, is why I want to do this book."

> *"Science can be an enormous help to people who are struggling with their faith. Most people who don't believe in God do so for so-called 'commonsense' reasons. Well, I'm sorry to have to tell them, but the commonsense world we all spend our time in doesn't exist.*

"Yes," I said. "That's why I want to do it too."

"That's good news. Because despite what you usually hear, science can be an enormous help to people who are struggling with their faith. Most people who don't believe in God do so for so-called 'commonsense' reasons. Well, I'm sorry to have to tell them, but the commonsense world we all spend our time in doesn't exist. Actually, I'm happy to tell them that. It's sort of a 'Go Tell It on the Mountain' kind of thing. It's a total fantasy that's been foisted on us by certain members of the scientific community, and we accept it because the scientific discoveries that could free us from this fantasy have taken place in regions far too small, and far too large, for our ordinary tools of perception, and our ordinary ways of thinking, to understand.

"Our eyes can't see quantum interactions. They can't see subatomic particles banging against one another, or coming into and out of existence. And, for that matter, our minds can't even envision them. These events take place on a level that we are not equipped to perceive, or even fully understand, in the commonsense way we understand how one ball on a pool table knocks another ball into a pocket. We, both of us right now, are immersed in the Zero Point Field, but neither of us can see or feel it. A fact like this, to most people, feels like a hopelessly abstract fantasy—something which, even if it is true, has nothing to do with their day-to-day lives.

"But make no mistake: it's *that* world, not the ordinary, commonsense one we think we're living in, that's the real one."

"And knowing this can help us," I said.

"Enormously!" said Bernie. "To become aware of the realities of our universe, the realities revealed by science only in recent, and sometimes *very* recent, years—this can offer us tremendous help in understanding our lives, and ourselves. Most important, knowing about that world can help pump genuine meaning back into life. We have this idea—because it's fed to us constantly—that science has robbed the world of meaning. But science hasn't done that. In fact, the situation is just the opposite. Science is an aid to faith, not a hindrance to it."

I thought I understood what he was getting at. Human beings are spiritual beings first and physical beings second. Our physicality is important, in the context of our navigating this current world as the physical beings we plainly are. But in the end, the physical world is an illusion. It's just not there. God *lends* the world its garment of solidity, just as he lends us everything else. You may own the biggest diamond in the world, but that diamond is nothing more than a swirling mass of energy disguising itself as something solid. The one genuine reality, the one true rock of realness amid all this vast, whirling, roiling sea of supercharged nothingness, is something else altogether.

> *I thought I understood what he was getting at. Human beings are spiritual beings first and physical beings second. Our physicality is important, in the context of our navigating this current world as the physical beings we plainly are. But in the end, the physical world is an illusion.*

"If matter isn't real," I asked Bernie, "what *is* real? Does anything," I asked, ripping off Little Feat, "really exist at all?"

"Absolutely," said Bernie.

"What?" I asked.

"We'll get to that," he said.

Down the hall, Marsha was seeing her pupil to the door. She poked her head in and asked if we were ready for something to eat.

"So," said Marsha. "Have you guys put together a bestseller in there yet?"

It had, of course, been my work on *Proof of Heaven* that had made Bernie interested in me as someone who could help him bring his message to a larger audience. I was confident that I could do so, but I was also anxious that things stayed in perspective.

I told Marsha that though I was proud of the work I'd done on *Proof of Heaven*, helping to transform a four-hundred-page manuscript into a slim page-turner, Eben's story was so extraordinary that it basically sold itself.

"Turning particle physics into a pulse-pounding page-turner," I said, "is going to be a little more challenging. But even though it's a stretch to say that Bernie has a 'popular' message, I think it's an important one that will connect with readers. There have been way too many bestsellers by writers who do a sloppy job of preaching that God doesn't exist. The world needs more books by non-sloppy scientists who believe He does."

I asked Marsha if she'd read *Proof of Heaven*.

"Yes, I did," she said. "And it rang a lot of bells. When I was sixteen, I had a near-death experience during my spring break from high school. My family—my father, Rankin, my mother, Mildred, and my sister, Marian, and I—were visiting some friends who we had a vacation share with at Rio del Mar, just south of Santa Cruz. The Wrights had two boys about Marian's and my age, and we four decided to wade out into the ocean and body surf.

"We were having a grand time until a large wave crashed over me, pulled me under, and then swept me out to sea. I was terrified, seeing the shore grow further and further away, and I screamed to my friends for help, and soon our parents ran out to see what all the commotion was about. As I drifted further out, something totally unexpected took place.

"I gradually slipped into a strangely relaxed state, and another reality suddenly descended on me. It felt like I was now existing in a realm between life and death. Several of my relatives who had died and passed on to the other side appeared around me, holding me afloat in what felt like a sumptuous halo of love. I saw my grandmother Blanche Sims, my grandfather James Sims, my great-grandmother Elizabeth Sims; my grandmother Rose Michaelis and my grandfather John Michaelis. I think there were more ancestors going back several hundred years, but I didn't recognize them, just felt they were there, and that they were related to me. They spoke to me mentally and said, 'Don't worry, we will hold you afloat until rescue arrives. It's not time for you to die yet.'

"I felt like I was flooded with love—almost drowning in it, just as, moments before, I felt I was drowning in the water. I was in such an altered emotional state that even though I was a good swimmer, I didn't feel the need to swim to keep afloat. I just put my head back in the water and floated.

"Eventually, a surfer managed to paddle out to where I was and helped me climb onto his surfboard. He took us in a direction perpendicular to the current that had swept me out, and then swung us around in a circular pattern until we reached the beach. He really knew what he was doing. Meanwhile my father had attempted to rescue me by going out in an inner tube, but was immediately swept in an opposite direction from us. A second surfer went after him, and got him back to shore using a similar strategy to the one that the surfer who rescued me used. It was certainly a lesson in how little I understood about how the ocean works. These surfers seemed to be doing things that made no sense, paddling in what seemed a direction that would lead us further out to sea. Yet they knew the currents, and how a stream of water that might seem to be taking you out to sea will eventually circle around and take you right back to land. They were precisely the people who needed to be at the beach that day, to bring both my father and me safely back to shore.

"As good as I felt when I was out there, my body was actually in very bad shape. I had hypothermia, and had to soak in a tub of hot water for about an hour before I stopped shaking. Gradually the feeling of peace and presence receded, and I turned back into what I was: a teenager who had barely escaped drowning. It turned out the ocean currents were extremely strong that day, and unfortunately another person was swept out to sea and drowned not far from where I'd been. I'm extremely grateful not only that those surfers were there, but that I was able to be open to the love that kept me afloat."

CHAPTER 8

Stardom

AFTER LUNCH, I went for a walk in the curious mix of upscale suburban streets and scenic marshland that the Haisches were situated amid. (They'd bought the house before the dot-com boom, and were among a scattering of ordinary people mixed in with the start-up millionaires who'd mostly taken over the area.) If I squinted hard through the midday sun, I could see distant office buildings where, of course, I pictured scores of computer geeks staring at their screens, typing code.

Thinking about how much the concept of solidity—the question of what was genuinely real and solid, and what was airy and fleeting—had figured in our morning talk, and about the fact that Bernie was, above all else, a guy *who studied stars*, got me to thinking on another kind of star, and the curious relationship I'd had with this kind, during my years working at

Guideposts, an inspirational magazine with a largely Christian readership, founded by Norman Vincent Peale in 1949.

Say the word "star" to the average American, and he or she will most likely think not of the celestial but of the human kind—the celebrities which our country has long led the world in being obsessed with.

Living in New York City, as I had for fifteen years, including the nine I'd spent at the magazine, makes you aware of how eager people—at least people on the two coasts—are to be famous. It would sometimes seem to me like the city was composed of two distinct varieties of people: the famous, and those who wanted to be famous.

A few years into the nine I spent at *Guideposts*, a decision was made to begin to place stars on the cover, rather than the ordinary folk who, up to then, had usually been featured.

Intrigued by this new turn of events, I decided to make an effort to try and interest some genuine stars in the magazine and organize some interviews with them.

I did this in large part out of curiosity. Basically, it seemed to me that the real reason so many people craved stardom was because they felt it would confer on them an expanded sensation of existence—of being *real*. In a world like ours, where belief in God was so weak in comparison to what it had been in centuries past, I felt that fame, stardom, was a kind of substitute for the feeling of genuinely existing in God's eyes that had been so much more easily had in the days when faith was stronger.

In times past, this feeling of being *real*, of having a genuine, lasting spiritual identity in addition to one's passing physical one, was considered a gift that God conferred on humans by creating them. Now, however, especially in centers of secularism like New York, it seemed like this feeling was not available without the benefit of the media, the Internet, and all the other modern technological crutches that now existed for creating an instant, if fleeting, sense of lastingness and genuine importance in the cosmos.

I have a friend who is related to a very famous actor. She once asked him, shortly after he had become a household name, what this felt like. Was there a real feeling of satisfaction that came with it?

His response was fascinating. He told her that being famous didn't really hit that inner target that we all imagine it will. And yet, he told her, the thing about fame was that once you have some, it becomes like a drug. Though it doesn't really satisfy you, you want more.

Thanks to *Guideposts'* new star drive, I felt like I had a chance to investigate this phenomenon at close hand.

It all turned out to be a lot easier than I'd thought. Before long, a few judicious phone calls and a pitch about the magazine's large circulation got me hooked up for interviews with genuine, bona fide stars.

The first one was with George Foreman. With his days of boxing behind him, Foreman was now a licensed minister, and ran a church deep in the Fifth Ward of Houston, the same rough neighborhood that he'd grown up in. This made him a good fit for *Guideposts*, which focused on how faith could help surmount life's challenges.

After an hour of driving deeper and deeper into what was clearly a very impoverished part of the city (each house I passed seemed to have a pit bull on a chain in the yard), I found Foreman's church. Along with the youth center he'd built just down the road for local kids to work out in, the church stood like a strange oasis in the midst of all the low-income houses around it.

Foreman himself, whom I interviewed in his church, was easygoing and, as I'd figured, extremely likable. But what truly took me by surprise was the way I felt once the interview was done. Foreman's presence was so imposing, he was so clearly a person of intense substance, that for the rest of that day and the day after, I was nagged by a strange, and unpleasant, sense of my own flimsiness. Despite Foreman's charm and courtesy, the sheer density of his celebrity left me feeling like a little of my own core, my own sense of self, had been depleted.

The same phenomenon, mostly to a lesser extent, occurred with the other celebrities I tracked down and interviewed for the magazine. Whether I was hanging out for the afternoon with a jovial Billy Ray Cyrus (while a then very young Miley played about at our feet) or conducting a deeply surreal one-on-one interview with Dolly Parton in a big empty office at Dollywood, I would return from these celebrity sojourns with my spiritual batteries consistently, and inexplicably, depleted.

None of this was the stars' fault. All the ones I interviewed while at *Guideposts* were uniformly polite, uniformly genial. There was just something about the simple fact of their fame that left me weak and mildly depressed for several days after meeting them.

After a year or so of this, I eased myself off the star beat and went back to interviewing the farmers, firemen, and housewives who were the magazine's staple fare. But the memory of my year or so of consistent star exposure stayed with me. There was, I felt, something to be learned from it, though it took me some time to figure out what that something was.

We call stars "stars" because of a very, very old human idea; one that dates back as far as ancient Egypt. In a nutshell, this idea is that the stars in the sky above represent the souls of individuals who have navigated the field of life and ascended into a higher world. They now look down on us and encourage us as we struggle along through our earthly journey.

"We are stardust, we are golden," sing Crosby, Stills & Nash in the opening scenes of the film *Woodstock*, as the young people with their blankets and their sleeping bags all stumble toward what, at the time, they imagine to be a new society, free of all the rules and hypocrisies of the one they grew up in. This image of stars as humans who have navigated the obstacle course of life and ascended to heaven is ingrained even in our flag, where, according to some scholars, the stripes symbolize the "horizontal" world of earthly life, while the stars in the blue of the flag's corner represent not just the states of the new republic, but the souls of those who have left the horizontal world of earthly life behind for the blue sky of the heavens above.

Stardom is so ingrained in the American sensibility that you could say it is, in a way, our American religion. But the stardom we crave is not the cheap kind, not the fleeting, supermarket checkout kind, but something far grander. Deep within us, we have a vision of life as a kind of obstacle course which we must successfully navigate in order to gain entrance, at life's end, to heaven above.

We want to be stars because we want to rise, like the stars do each evening, above the struggle and pain of life on earth, and find our place in the sky above as true and lasting heavenly be-ings. "Look at me!" the growing child says to his or her mother and father, and on some level, many of us spend the rest of our lives repeating versions of this same demand. Though the one we are really addressing, in this desperate bid for attention, is, to state things straight out, God. Because we live in a culture that makes it harder and harder to see ourselves as existing in the hands of a benevolent creator who made us for a reason and has hopes and dreams for us, we have become a nation, and to some extent a world, of attention addicts.

What does this have to do with science, with what Bernie and I had been discussing that morning?

Everything. For the chief reason we are no longer able to feel ourselves as genuinely existing in the eyes of a God who created us for an eternal life with Him is . . . science. Or rather, what is presented to us as science, but which is all too often mere opinion masquerading as science.

This all made me think of that other great American love—sports. Back in my days at Potomac, I was miserable at sports, and deeply resented all the hours I was made to spend running about chasing balls of various kinds, when I would much rather have been at home reading or watching TV. Yet of all those bleak, after-school afternoons playing football, or soccer, or capture the flag, or whatever pointless exercise was foisted on me, one day stands out in my memory.

During a game of football, the other side kicked the ball and it magically made its way through the air right into my arms. I prepared for it to bounce off my chest and hit the ground, as it usually did, but this time, improbably, I found myself holding it.

Here, for all intents and purposes, was a new situation. A game was going on, the ball was in play, and I had it.

For a second or two, I did what was expected of me. I clowned about, blithely ignoring the screamed pleas of my teammates to pass the ball to them.

But then, out of the blue, a strange new impulse took over. I decided to head for the end zone.

This was greeted with more groans from my teammates. The decent thing to do, after all, would have been to quickly toss the ball to one of the more talented members of the team, who might have had a chance of making it some ways down the field. But, fueled perhaps by the absolute certainty of my teammates that I wouldn't get anywhere, I set myself to running toward the distant end zone.

Members of the opposing team charged toward me. I ducked one, then another, then another. As the remaining players headed toward me, I picked up speed and, momentarily jettisoning all my smart-aleck disdain for sport in all its forms, charged like crazy for the end zone.

I made it. And in that one moment, I got a taste of something to do with sports that I'd never picked up on before. *Moving down the field has something to be said for it.*

Now, thinking about all these far-flung ideas, I realized why I was thinking about them. Though Bernie and I had spent our time that morning talking about substance in the cosmic sense—that is, what substance is, and whether it actually even exists in the universe—in the background there lurked another question that we had not yet broached.

What did all this talk of substance have to do with the question of *human* substance—of the deep and desperate need that all of us have for the knowledge that we really and truly *exist*? That we are real in a more than passing, *here-today-gone-tomorrow* kind of way?

I suddenly had an idea of what Bernie might have been hinting at when, at the end of our talk, I'd asked him what was real and he'd told me we'd get to that. I was now anxious to do just that.

CHAPTER 9

Simulation

*T*HIS IS ALL *going pretty well*, I thought to myself as I headed
back toward the Haisches, relying on my iPhone, as usual, to
navigate me through Redwood City's confusingly loopy and
roundabout suburban streets. In our first in-person encounter,
Bernie and I had seemed to be pretty much constantly finish-
ing each other's sentences. That was good news. The other
good news was that I had decided on the first of my Keys. It
emerged naturally from what Bernie had had to say about the
apparent reality of the physical world, and the truth that lay
beneath it:

> *The physical world is not real. It is not substantive. It feels*
> *that way, and it looks that way, but it isn't. There's nothing*
> *in it, because there's no such thing as solid matter.*

Once I got back to the house, Bernie and I sat down for our second talk of the day. Bernie instantly shot down all my optimistic feelings about how things were going by launching, seemingly out of nowhere, into a speech about the extraordinary advances that were being made in virtual reality machines.

"The virtual reality games available today," Bernie told me, "are truly amazing in comparison to the primitive, Mario Bros.–type games of the early eighties. Nowadays games and films using computer-generated images are strikingly realistic. Soon," he said, "there are going to be suits you step into that will take you to faraway worlds that will appear every bit as real as this one. Actually a lot of early models of these suits exist already, and it's incredibly exciting how well they work. Give it a few more years, and there's no telling how advanced the technology will get."

"Okay," I said, wondering how to negotiate this apparent interruption of craziness into what had looked like it was going to be a totally smooth process, "I get that you're excited about all this computer simulation stuff, and I'm sure it's very interesting, but I'm not sure what it has to do with our subject. I mean, what's the reality of God got to do with some guy getting into a suit and pretending he's climbing Mount Everest when he's just in some little white room?"

Bernie thought for a moment. I wasn't sure if he was trying to figure out what to say to put me at ease, or if he was just preparing to rail on some more about how great today's computer simulation technology was.

"The reason," he finally said, "that I'm so interested in the advances that virtual reality technology is making is because I see it as a model for how God created this universe."

"You mean," I said, half relieved and half still on my guard, "you see our universe as some kind of giant video game?"

"That's simplifying quite a bit, but yes. Basically, I believe that everything we see around us right now is a simulation. Entanglement, Einstein's spooky action at a distance—these seemingly unsolvable quantum problems are problems no longer, if you simply follow the lead given by today's computer technology and see the universe as a giant program."

"Entanglement" and "spooky action at a distance" (the latter is simply Einstein's term for the phenomenon) were references to a discovery, first intuited by Einstein (who didn't like it and hoped it wasn't true), and later codified in a theory by the physicist John Bell. The theory states that our universe is non-local in nature. This has been interpreted to mean that space as distance or separation does not, on a subatomic level, exist. In the 1960s, Bell hypothesized an experiment involving two paired particles (you might call them brother and sister particles) that were linked in such a way that when one was made to move in a certain way, the other particle would react immediately, mirroring its sibling's actions with no time lag whatsoever.

If, Bell said, you took a brother and a sister particle and placed them at opposite ends of the universe, and made one of the particles spin in a certain direction, its partner over at the other end of the universe would *instantly* mirror its sibling's actions. In other words, these two particles would be in instantaneous communication, with absolutely no time whatsoever elapsing between the movement of the one particle and that of its sibling no matter what the distance of separation. Bell's Theorem, which laid out the specifics of his theory in the mathematical language used by physicists to describe the invisible realities they explore, appeared in 1964. It was widely disregarded until 1997, when an experiment was performed at the University of Geneva in which two photons seven miles apart were shown to react instantaneously to each other. Seven miles is not that big a distance, but it is big enough to demonstrate that, no matter how anyone felt about it, space was, in fact, at some level an illusion, just as Einstein had feared. The physicist Henry Stapp, a student of Heisenberg's, called the Bell's Theorem validation the single most profound discovery in the history of science. "This," said Bernie, "would seem to violate the laws of special relativity . . . and majorly!"

"Well," I said, "I'm willing to follow you on this, of course, but I have to interrupt with the usual problem. I don't understand how computer programs work. Not a clue. And maybe you could make it clear how Bell's discovery relates to this excitement of yours about them."

"You don't need to have much understanding of how computer programming works. All you really have to understand is the basic nature of digital reality, and the basic nature of digital reality is that it is *generated* —that is, it's created. It's not real, in and of itself. It appears real, at a certain level, but it isn't. It's constructed, using a certain set of rules.

"And in a computer program, space is simply not an issue. If the universe is a big computer simulation, every part is connected to every other part instantly. There is no actual separation in a computer simulation, just *apparent* separation. That is, it looks like separation if you're in the program, as we are, but if you're outside the program, as God is, then distance simply isn't an issue. Nor, for that matter, is time. If we see the universe as a giant computer program, we can understand how it is that certain atomic events, like a radioactive atom emitting an electron very precisely, again and again, over a certain period of time, can happen. The proton or neutron doesn't know when to leave the radioactive atom. But it doesn't need to, because the event is programmed to happen.

"But to get back to actually imagining how our world is very much like a giant computer-generated illusion, take a film like *Avatar.* The scenery in that film looks wonderfully, impressively real and organic. Yet every inch of it represents thousands of bits of computer code, translated using enormously complex sets of algorithms into a series of colored dots that come together to imitate what we experience as reality. But of course, the reality of a scene in *Avatar* is numbers and code, nothing else.

"Now, how did that code come together to produce this illusion? It's thanks to the work of hundreds upon hundreds of people, devoting their intelligence and skills to this single project of fooling your eye into seeing something that isn't there. So ultimately, though virtual realities can seem incredibly real, if you go back far enough, you will eventually find something, or some One, who has constructed this artificial reality, and who *is* real."

"Okay," I said, "so you and I are sitting, right now, in a digital office, with digital books on the digital shelves, and stacks of digital papers about to fall off that digital desk over there. And I'm seeing that digital stack of about-to-collapse papers using digital eyes, set in a digital skull, that is part of my digital body?"

"Oops," Bernie said, quickly glancing over his shoulder.

"Just kidding about the stack of papers," I said.

"Yes," said Bernie, "In conventional computing systems, all information is stored using a binary system—that is, a system of two numbers: one and zero. Everything in the computer world, ultimately, goes back to those two numbers. It turns out that the simple binary of 'one' and 'zero' is so good at preserving information that it's just a matter of time before we will be able to capture and replicate the entire surface of the earth and everything on it just by using ones and zeros. A hundred years ago no one would have imagined this. Even fifty years ago, the computer power used in the manned Apollo moon missions was about a million times less than one of today's smartphones. We are rushing toward a world of simulation that will be truly staggering by any measure. And the more staggering it is, the clearer it will be that God may use similar techniques to construct the virtual world we are living in right now."

"Back in Nyack," I said, "there's a record shop that just opened—something I'd never have expected would happen just a year or two ago. Young people are going back to vinyl records because there's that natural sound to them, that warmth, as everyone says, that digital will never be able to replicate, because when you get down to it, CDs are composed, like computer programs, of ones and zeroes, so there's a certain essential smoothness to recorded music that digital is always going to miss.

"But what you're telling me—and I must say, it feels kind of weird—is that nature, the whole outside world around us, is more like a CD than a vinyl record. *Nature, in short, is digital.* When you get down small enough, everything in our world is composed of discrete little 'bits,' like the dots in a newspaper photograph. Nature, if you go down small enough, is not smooth and slippery. It's composed of tiny little building blocks that are absolutely discrete."

"That's right," he said.

"So you could say that, essentially, the ultimate building blocks of nature, of matter, of the whole world around us, are discrete 'bits' of information, or 'quanta' [the plural of 'quantum'], that are not all that different, in the way they work, from the individual bits of information that go into a CD or a computer program."

"Yes," said Bernie. "That's all correct. A quantum is a completely distinct entity. So the quantum world really *can* be envisioned using a computer analogy, because computers use a binary system of individual ones and zeroes, and the quantum world moves in discrete jumps, rather than in a smooth, uninterrupted way.

"And as you say, it's like looking at a newspaper photograph. From a distance, there are flowing lines, all kinds of different smooth shapes, shades of light and dark. But if you zero in, you discover that all those smooth lines and subtle shades are really individual dots, with no smooth lines and surfaces at all. The quantum world is like that. It's all bits."

"And that's this world around us?" I asked.

"Yes," said Bernie. "That's this world around us."

"Okay," I said. "I know where you're going now. This world around us isn't real. We're living, for all intents and purposes, in the next James Cameron film. Nothing around is actually real, actually solid. It's a simulation, created using 'bits' of information that are similar to the bits of information used in computer code. I got it. And I can guess what the next question is going to be, and what the answer to that question is going to be. But before I get to that, I think we need to clear out some problematic implications of the computer analogy."

"Indeed we do," said Bernie. "In fact, comparisons between computer programming and the nature of physical reality have led to what I see as an extremely dangerous idea: that people—both their bodies and their minds—will eventually be uploaded onto computers. That, to me, is deeply sinister. But it gets quite a bit worse than that. The *New York Times* recently published an article called 'Our Lives, Controlled from Some Guy's Couch.'"

"Let me guess," I said. "It suggested that our whole world is just an elaborate program generated by some computer geek far in the future."

"Exactly," said Bernie.

"Well, that's about the most horrible idea I've heard in a while."

"Yes," said Bernie. "It would be the ultimate dreadful validation of the mechanistic model of what human beings are. We would really and truly turn out to be nothing but vast collections of data. We would be digital versions of the brain in the vat, bubbling along. It's an almost inconceivably horrid thought."

"But," I said, "you don't believe any of that, obviously."

"No, I certainly don't," said Bernie. "What I believe is that instead of using advances in computer technology to downgrade human beings to batches of data, we can instead use that technology to point us in a very different direction. A direction that leads to something both obvious, yet deeply significant: If you have a highly sophisticated digital simulation, you also find, if you look far enough back, a programmer."

"And that programmer," I said, "is not some kid on a couch."

"It sure isn't," said Bernie. "The virtual worlds we move through were created . . ."

"By God," I said, happy to finish his sentence for him.

"Yes," said Bernie. "That's what I think at least. But the question then arises: What tools did he use to make this fantastically real virtual universe? We've spent a lot of time talking about how this seemingly solid physical world isn't solid at all. So when it comes to creating this vast simulation that the universe in fact is, we have to ask: What materials did God use to create it? God didn't use hardware to create our virtual world. How could he, when, as we've seen, in the real world, which is God's world, there's no such thing as solid material?"

"So," I said, "I know that the virtual world we're all so wrapped up in today, though it all appears wonderfully immaterial, is in fact served by tremendous amounts of very real, very solid machinery. Acres of humming servers, jillions of miles of cable, etc, etc. So I guess what I'm saying is: I get how God could construct all this great software to cook up this digital world we live in. But . . . the analogy starts to fail, for me, when I try to envision how this could be done in a world where none of that hardware exists."

"Well," said Bernie, "the analogy only goes so far. And it is, let's be clear, an analogy. From our talk on the Zero Point Field earlier, you've come to see, I think, that the whole idea of solid material is an illusion. So God, in creating our virtual world, couldn't use material means to do so, because there aren't any. But the great thing is, he wouldn't *need* any solid matter to create the universe. Remember: Solid matter isn't solid. Physical solidity of any kind is a myth. So you need to start with that weird, but nonetheless true, fact in your mind. So if we are bending our heads, trying to imagine a set of conditions that, quite frankly, are beyond our capacity to imagine, we can nonetheless hypothesize that, in order to create our world, God would need, the way I see it, two things."

"What are they?"

"The first thing," said Bernie, "is mathematics. Our world is profoundly mathematical. The astrophysicist Mario Livio, in his book *Is God a Mathematician?*, explored this in some detail. He's not the first person to do so. Many deep thinkers have. The fact is, God's mathematical handprint is all over the universe. The astrophysicist Sir James Jeans suggested that the universe appears to have been designed by what he calls a 'pure mathematician.' I'm convinced that mathematics was one of the key inventions God used to create our universe. We take the mathematical laws that govern this universe for granted. We know that two plus two equals four, for example, and don't give it another thought. But in doing so, we do God a profound disservice, for in fact, it is thanks to God that two and two in fact do equal four. We could just as easily live in a universe where two and two equal five."

"Okay," I said, "that makes no sense."

"Of course it doesn't," said Bernie. "After all, how could a universe where two plus two equals five make sense to a creature like you, who inhabits a universe where two plus two equals four?"

"But," I said, "I just have no comprehension how such a thing as that could be."

"Again," said Bernie, "of course you don't, because you live in this particular universe, which operates according to rules of mathematics, rules of logic, which you've known all your life and take for granted. But you shouldn't take them for granted, because God created them."

I was beginning to cotton on to what Bernie was telling me, and its marvelous beauty. I had grown up assuming that the rules of the world I lived in were just "there," with no need to question them. But this wasn't so. When God created this universe, he created every aspect of it, right down to the rules of logic and mathematics that most of us take completely for granted.

> *When God created this universe, he created every aspect of it, right down to the rules of logic and mathematics that most of us take completely for granted.*

"One of the great discoveries you make when you become a scientist," Bernie said, "or at least a believing scientist, is just how much more we have to be grateful for than we know. We used to assume that everything is just as it is, and that it could be no other way. In fact, exactly the opposite is the case. There is nothing in our universe, nothing in the world we wake up to every day, that couldn't be different. That couldn't easily not exist at all.

"God gets all the credit for everything in our universe, and that extends not just to the grass and the clouds, and the people and animals we love, but to the most seemingly ordinary and obvious rules of how things in the world around us work. The truly scientific attitude to have toward our world is to under-stand that nothing in it just happens to be as it is. Everything—absolutely everything—in it could have been different. And that is most especially the case with the other ingredient that, along with mathematics, God used to create our world."

"And that other ingredient is?" I asked.

"Consciousness," said Bernie. "Consciousness is the ulti-mate building block of our universe. Nothing could happen without consciousness. It is God's greatest, and most mysteri-ous, gift to us."

We had come, with that word, to the heart of the matter.

"Images on a computer screen, after all, are really just what happens when electronics carry out a computer code. Similarly, imagine some part of God's consciousness creating a virtual universe using his thoughts. He has no need for electronics. Using his vast code (The Universe, version 1.0), God can create a totally realistic simulation. His consciousness can handle all of that. Instead of electronic bytes madly racing around in a computer, his thoughts can do all that. And what is the purpose of this? To create a virtual world for us. The notion that the world is a dream, maya, or illusion is correct. And now we know how it's done: God's consciousness emulates a vast computer . . . just a bit more powerful (well, actually a lot more powerful) than the ones creating Hollywood films.

CHAPTER 10

Consciousness

W ITH THE WORD "consciousness" introduced into the conversation, I suddenly realized why our morning talk had got me
thinking about my days at *Guideposts*, with our modern world's
obsession with fame, and with that feeling of fleeting reality
that I believed so many people in the modern world suffered
from.

I also realized that with it, we had stepped to the very center
of what our discussions had been moving toward from the very
beginning.

"Consciousness" is a notoriously hard word to define, but
one simple—and accurate—way to do so is to substitute another
word for it: thought.

The word "thought" took on new significance when the

seventeenth-century philosopher and scientist René Descartes used it in what is perhaps the single most famous philosophical statement in history.

This sentence, *Cogito ergo sum*, is usually translated as "I think, therefore I am." It's one that most people remember from school no matter how little contact with Philosophy classes they may have had.

Though Descartes first formulated this sentence in Latin, he introduced it to the world in 1644 in his native French as *Je pense, donc je suis*. But whatever language this sentence is spoken in, its meaning remains clear: the fact that we think is evidence—incontrovertible evidence—that we exist.

Thinking, said Descartes, is the one and only thing, in a world where we must greet everything we see with doubt and a demand for proof, *that does not require proof*. It does not require proof because it is self-evident. No one can doubt that he or she thinks—that he or she is conscious. This is, said Descartes, the one unqualified truth that we can know—the one fact that is evident without any need of experiment.

But a closer look at Descartes's famous declaration reveals another message: to arrive at truth, we must separate our minds from everything else in the universe.

Descartes, in short, is the father of our distinctly modern way of looking at the world: as a collection of material objects that we can isolate, measure, perform experiments on, and just generally treat as separate objects; objects having nothing to do with the thinking, watching, manipulating selves that are per-forming all these experiments.

For Descartes, the division between the *out there* world of objects and the *in here* world of thought was firm. This divi-sion in essence launched modern science, for it freed scientists to measure, weigh, kill, dissect, experiment on, and just basically do whatever it wanted to the world and all the things, be they living or dead, within it.

In the world before Descartes, objects could be loaded down with all kinds of invisible yet real qualities. A holy relic pre-served in a church was holy not just because it had, at some point in the past, been associated with a sacred event. That holiness lived, as a very real power, within that object itself.

Not so after Descartes. By dividing the world into "inner" and "outer," he robbed the outer world not just of its holiness, but of all qualities, from large to small.

Before Descartes came along, the world was full of quali-ties. After Descartes, all those qualities were swept away as mere illusion. If a particular spot—a section of woods, say—held a certain kind of magic that all who went there could feel, people understood it as special. After Descartes, there was nothing real about this so-called magic. The leaves on the trees were real. The earth those trees grew out of was real. But all moods and atmospheres, all beauty, anything at all that failed the test of being physically analyzable, was proclaimed unreal. This even extended to color, which Descartes proclaimed was a creation of the "inside" world of the mind, and was not present at all in the nuts-and-bolts, measurable world, with which science was from then on exclusively to concern itself.

In 1665, just a few decades after Descartes formulated his famous sentence, an outbreak of bubonic plague sent the young scholar Isaac Newton back from Cambridge University to Woolsthorpe, the English country manor where the wealthy young man had grown up. While reading under an apple tree in his family's orchard, Newton watched an apple drop from the tree to the ground. (This story is often told with the apple landing squarely on Newton's head, but that part was added later.)

This seemingly obvious observation led Newton to ask a question that no one, in the history of humanity, had apparently asked before. Why, Newton wondered, did that apple make a beeline for the ground instead of—who knows?—drifting off into the countryside, or floating up into the sky?

For the same reason, Newton swiftly intuited, that he himself, and every other object around him, didn't drift off into the sky. Something was holding both him, the apple, and everything else down.

This observation led Newton to suggest the existence of gravity, the first and most important of those invisible forces that Bernie and I had begun our conversations discussing.

Along with a handful of other men—Galileo, Copernicus, and, a century later, Charles Darwin—Descartes and Newton created the world we live in today: a world full of physical objects that seem real, and an inner world of thought, or consciousness, which is not real.

It should be mentioned, by the way, that this was not Descartes's original intent. By separating the inner world of thought, or consciousness, from the outer world of measurable things, Descartes merely meant to divide the world into two parts: the *res extensa*, or exterior world, and the *res cogitans*, or the inner world of thought. Like all the other fathers of modern science, Descartes was a firm believer in God.

But by the beginning of the twentieth century, scientists had pretty much forgotten about granting the inner world of thought, or consciousness, any kind of reality. What was the point? By treating the exterior world as a dead realm of matter to be manipulated and used however we liked, science had made tremendous advances, changing the entire world more in a few hundred years than it had been changed in all the thousands of years that had elapsed before its sudden explosive birth.

"Okay," I said, back in Bernie's office. "I have a feeling that consciousness is the up-to-now invisible planet that, whether we meant to or not, we've both been circling closer and closer to. 'Consciousness,' frustratingly vague a word as it is, is the word that lies at the center of everything we've been talking about. And in line with that, I think now I understand where you've been heading with all of these arguments you've been putting forth so far. The model that you were given, that I was given, in Science class when we were kids was that consciousness was something that only came into existence with life. Most likely it came only with quite advanced life. For the billions of years before life arose in the universe, there was no consciousness. Primitive life appeared, but there was no consciousness to be aware of these events, because consciousness only arose after brains developed. First animal, then human brains, which, through the sparks of the synapses zipping back and forth within those brains, created this thing we know as consciousness."

"Exactly," said Bernie. "And because the phenomenon of consciousness has been sold short, ordinary people who look to science for answers are sold short too. Because consciousness didn't arise from matter. It wasn't created by brains. Consciousness is . . ."

"Primary," I said, glad that I was back to completing Bernie's sentences for him. "Consciousness didn't 'arise.' It was here from the beginning. It was, in fact, the first thing, from which all else arose."

"And that," Bernie said, "is the reason I'm excited by computers. Not because we're all living in some computer program created by a bored kid on his couch two hundred years from now, creepily imaginative as that idea is. But because we are conscious beings, living in a simulated universe that was itself created by a conscious being—the supreme conscious being.

"There is nothing genuinely real in our world save for one thing: and that 'thing' (which, of course, isn't a thing) is consciousness. All virtual worlds are, if you follow them back far enough, created. At the end of the day, as they say, the virtual world—its rules, the algorithms thanks to which it is able to run—cannot be created by anything that lives within that same virtual domain. It must be created by something, or Someone, which is outside it and above it.

"Consciousness is, to use your analogy about music, the one true 'analog' phenomenon in the universe. Nothing else is genuinely fluid, nothing else is able to transcend the 'virtual' nature of everything else in the universe. There is, in fact, nothing else in the world that truly exists. Everything real is consciousness."

And with that, I realized, I had my second Key:

Consciousness is the only reality in our universe. Matter, energy, space . . . All these things are only simulations, generated by God using the sole and single "thing" in this universe that actually exists. The world of objects we move through is not conscious, but we are. And because we are conscious, we are real.

Emerging from that second talk with Bernie into the overwhelming normalcy of Bernie and Marsha's house, with the sounds of yet another singing lesson going on upstairs, I marveled at the way these talks had of pulling me into another frame of mind.

There was, I realized, something so real about the things Bernie was saying that, at least while we were discussing them, they had what bordered on a physical effect on me. For all the griping I'd done about my sorry situation in life recently, I was in a truly privileged situation. I was talking with one of those rare individuals who could actually speak, with real authority, about what I really was, about what the world around me really was, and what it all meant. Bernie was, slowly but surely, pulling me into his understanding of the world. And it was doing what I'd hoped it would do, but secretly doubted that it could.

It was cheering me up.

I noticed that Bernie, like me, was one of those people who was happiest when engaged in something, and would sort of pop out of gear and not know what to do with himself when he wasn't busy. Bernie and Marsha ate dinner early, and once it was done, and Marsha had brought Pogo, their pet box turtle, in for the night, and Bernie had settled himself in front of CNN, I found myself sorely challenged for how to get through the night. That night—my second at the Haisches'—I shut my door, settled my six-foot-two frame somewhat haphazardly into Taylor's bed, and waited for the two Ambien I'd taken to kick in.

Here I am, I thought, *in the middle of Silicon Valley, and I've just found out that I live in a giant computer program created by God.*

And, meditating on that peculiarity, I was out.

CHAPTER 11

Church

T HE FOLLOWING DAY— a Friday—Marsha declared that it would be fun for me to get a tour of San Francisco proper. I didn't much want to go as it seemed early in my stay to be indulging in tourist jaunts, but Marsha was persuasive, so with Bernie and me in tow, she marshaled us into her Lexus, and we headed for the city.

Like most big cities these days, San Francisco was choked with traffic, and for the trip in I spent much of my time (rudely, I knew) texting testily back and forth with Colleen. In the historic district, Marsha, after much looking, at last found a parking place, and we all trooped in to take a look at Mission Dolores, a Catholic church that is the oldest standing structure in San Francisco. While Marsha and Bernie busied themselves in the back of the church, I walked up to one of the front pews and sat down.

So here I was, for the first time since I'd started work on this book about God, in a church. Looking up at the classically grim, no-holds-barred Catholic Jesus nailed to his cross on the wall above the nave, I found myself thinking how funny it was that I, someone who thought constantly about God, so rarely set foot in a church.

It wasn't that I didn't consider myself a genuine Christian. In fact, for someone who thought of himself as existing at the borders of the faith, I was quite set in my ways when it came to certain questions of doctrine. When Bernie suggested that God was evolving, for example, I was quick to point out that this was a dangerous idea, leading toward process theology at best, and pantheism at worst. Perhaps because I had not set foot in one until I was ten, at which time I made a brief entrance into an Episcopal church in Boston for my sister's wedding, my discomfort in churches simply had to do with the fact that I was unfamiliar with them.

However I ended up the way I am, it seemed to me that a book on the inevitable collision of religion and science was probably best written by someone whose faith was an odd and eccentric one, as mine was. Most of my New York friends were atheists or, at best, agnostics. The books I wrote, all of which were in one way or another on spiritual topics, were treated by most of my friends as an eccentricity—something that, inexplicable and mildly embarrassing as they were, could be overlooked because I was, in other ways, a normal enough person.

I was certain that the imminent collision between faith and science would not rob Christianity, or other religions, of their core identities. The coming change was not one where either religion or science would "win," but one, rather, in which a Sunday worshipper *or* a scientist in a lab could go about his or her business without the small, nagging voice that was now whispering in so many ears, both of believers and unbelievers. This was the voice that said: "Either religion is wrong, or science is wrong. They cannot both be right."

And yet I knew, with an assurance I couldn't completely explain, that this voice was wrong. When an advocate of the "New Atheism," the intellectual movement birthed by authors like Richard Dawkins and Christopher Hitchens, would remark, in the face of any real understanding of history, that religion was responsible for all the bad things that had ever happened in the course of humankind's time on earth, I would marvel, but not just for the obvious reasons. I would marvel not just at how such a wrongheaded remark could be made by an accomplished scientist or a respected public intellectual. I would marvel because such comments were so far from the real, beating heart of the issue.

Albert Einstein, someone with the genuine credentials to speak on these matters, once famously said that "the most beautiful thing we can experience is the mysterious. It is the source of all true art and science. He to whom the emotion is a stranger, who can no longer pause to wonder and stand rapt in awe, is as good as dead—his eyes are closed. The insight into the mystery of life, coupled though it be with fear, has also given rise to religion. To know that what is impenetrable to us really exists, manifesting itself as the highest wisdom and the most radiant beauty, which our dull faculties can comprehend only in their most primitive forms—this knowledge, this feeling is at the center of true religiousness."

In this passage, Einstein is essentially saying as a scientist what Robert Frost said as a poet: We dance round in a ring and suppose (and conduct experiments, and devise brilliant theories), but the "Secret" sits in the middle, the center, and knows. This "place" is where all true science and religion point, and it emanates a fundamental mystery that, no matter how much we know of it, we will never completely capture.

It was my recognition of this sense of wonder that, in a childish yet nonetheless earnest way, made me grumble through my alternative version of the Lord's Prayer during those morning assemblies of my school days, rather than give praise to a God I didn't recognize. It was this same recognition of wonder that, thanks to C. S. Lewis and then to other authors, brought me back, with surprise, to a consideration of Christianity as a genuine avenue to this central mystery. And ultimately, it was the words of Jesus that I found in the Gospels that made me recognize, once and for all, that for me the true source of this wonder lay there.

Yet for all the earnestness of my embrace of Christianity,

I remained, in a fundamental sense, an outsider to it. I might never be truly comfortable in a church, but this was, in some ways, a good thing because it allowed me always to remain in touch with that sense of being a wanderer and a looker. I was an outsider to organized religions, just as I was an outsider to science. The one area where I was not an outsider was in that sense of wonder that Einstein talked about in that famous passage.

In a time when the established voices of both science and religion so often detract from what is genuinely true and important about the religion/science debate, that sense of wonder was, I felt, a compass point that one could always rely on. In the first two Keys Bernie had handed me the day before, I felt I had the first two steps to where I was going on this journey: steps that would lead, naturally and inevitably, to a third.

I was interrupted from these thoughts by Marsha, who bent over to tell me that she and Bernie were going outside. I followed, stopping on the way out to take a picture of a statue of the Virgin Mary that particularly appealed to me. Colleen, a Catholic, always liked the bare feet that images of the Virgin tended to have. Thanks to a feeling of generousness of spirit that the visit to this church had imparted, I took a shot of this Virgin's conspicuously bare feet and texted it to Colleen.

We had planned to stay and have dinner in town, but Bernie was getting tired, and I told Marsha I'd seen enough of San Francisco and was ready to go back to good old Silicon Valley. On the way back the traffic was even worse than it had been coming in, and Marsha—an accomplished opera singer—asked me what I thought of opera.

"I hate it," I announced confidently. "I'm more of a Guns N' Roses kind of guy."

"Oh, well," said Marsha, "maybe you haven't given it a chance." Then, to my horror, she reached into the compartment between the two front seats and pulled out a CD.

"This is me singing the lead in a recent local production of *Carmen*," she announced. For the next half hour of bumper-to-bumper traffic, I listened to Marsha do what sounded like a bang-up job. Nonetheless, it remained opera, and I still hated opera.

"I've got some music here," I said, when a break in *Carmen* came up. "I wonder if I can plug my phone into your car's stereo system."

"That sounds like a great idea," Marsha said gamely. I had the Cult's live version of "Love Removal Machine" all cued up, but, sadly, was unable to get the car to connect with my phone, and so was left to wonder how Marsha would have fared at enduring it.

Once we got to our restaurant—a pizza place in Palo Alto, a couple towns south of Redwood City—we were told that there would be a short wait for a table. As Bernie, Marsha, and I stood outside the restaurant in the dimming light, I looked up and saw a single star.

"What star is that, Bernie?" I asked.

"What's what?" Bernie said, clearly a little worn out from the day.

"That star up there. Or is it Venus? It doesn't seem quite bright enough for Venus."

Bernie looked up, but couldn't make out the celestial body.

"You know," I said, "I've often read something that I still can't get my head around. It can take so long for the light of a star to travel to earth that the star itself might not even exist anymore."

"Well," said Bernie, "that is a popular fact among writers on these subjects. But the truth is actually a good bit weirder. Not only is your retina catching photons that may have left their particular light source millions of years ago, but the photons of light that are hitting your retina knew ahead of time that your retina would be here to catch them."

By this time I was pretty used to hearing totally nonsensical astrophysical facts. But I was still stopped short by this one.

"That's ridiculous," I said. "I mean, even more ridiculous than the average ridiculous. It's completely impossible."

"Only if you live in a world of objects that have no relation to each other," said Bernie. He was still tired, even if he didn't say so—Bernie was, I knew by this point, not one to remind you that he had a chronic disease—but not tired enough to miss a chance to give his universe-as-computer-simulation theory another plug.

"Remember, in a computer program, everything in the program is instantly connected to everything else. A photon knowing you'd be here to catch it with your eye is no problem, because in this universe, time—the time we're enduring now as we wait to get a seat at this pizza place—does not exist.

"Einstein's special theory of relativity states that there is infinite time dilation and length contraction for a particle traveling at the speed of light, i.e. a photon. According to Einstein, a photon of light cannot experience space or time."

"Bernie," I said, "I'm too tired to get hit with infinite time dilation."

"No, you're right," he said. "We don't need to get into that. Just imagine it like this. From the photon's point of view it doesn't just whizz though space from there (the star) to here (the retina of your eye) for who knows how many millions of years. It simply jumps in zero time from there to here. We live in a world where we have to deal with time and space. But that's because we're caught in the simulation. Get outside the simulation, and you'd see that what we experience as a photon's long trek across the universe is actually a single event; one that is essentially free of the time constraints that we, not being photons, have to suffer under.

"Of course, taking a photon's view is hard—impossible, in fact. What's it like to move at the speed of light? These are experiences that lie beyond us, because we are simply too big, and the apparatus we use to take in information—our eyes, our ears— are simply too big to be able to process information that's that small and that fast. All we can do is rely on mathematics to paint a picture of what it's like at that level of existence. But basically, in the world as it really is, as opposed to the (comparatively) very clumsy and imprecise level at which we experience it, the journey of a photon from point A to point B is not something that takes place in time as we understand it.

"The photon's departure from the star and its arrival on the retina of your eye is essentially a single action. Which it would be, also, if the universe is, as I maintain, essentially a giant computer program. If the universe is a computer program, distance as an issue is essentially done away with because distance is an illusion created by the program. So it is that the emission-absorption process—the journey from the star to the retina of your eye—becomes essentially one event rather than two—like an algorithm in a computer program."

"Well," I said, "that's actually not all that different from what theologians say when they describe God's view of time as similar to what we see when we look at a mountain range. God sees the whole spread of all that has happened and all that is to come. Because (though the theologians of course don't use this language) he's outside the program.

"So," I asked, grateful that Bernie had pulled me into his world and away from the tedium of waiting for our table to be called, "what if no one was here to see the light? What would happen if that photon had no place to land, if it had been doomed to travel forever through space without ever striking an object? What would it do then? Would it even bother to leave its source to begin with?"

"It's a good question," Bernie said. "It hasn't been tested, so far as I know, and I don't know that anyone will ever be able to."

"But there's a chance that, possibly, a photon could choose, if it knew that it would be doomed to travel forever, without ever hitting an object, not to leave the light source to begin with?"

"Sure," said Bernie. "We just don't know because we don't have the capacity to test what would happen."

I glanced up again at the distant star, now just a little clearer in the darkening sky than it had been moments before, and tried to process what Bernie had just told me. Again I felt that slight, marvelous disconnect between my mundane experience, standing in front of a pizza restaurant on a busy Northern California Friday evening, and the world as it actually was.

A world where time was an illusion, which I fell for because my senses and intellect were built in such a way that I was programmed to fall for it. And I saw once again how marvelous a tool science was in plugging me into the universe of brilliance and meaning all around me, and how sad it was that so many people thought it was a barrier to belief and wonder, rather than a door to it.

CHAPTER 12

As Above, So Below

"I've been thinking about it," I said to Bernie the next morning, after we'd set ourselves up in his study and I'd turned my phone on, "and I can see why you're so cautious about people writing about this Higgs and Zero Point Field stuff. When you were talking about them, I realized that both fields reminded me of something. I tried to think of what that 'something' was, and then it came to me. They reminded me of the Force in the original *Star Wars*.

"I'd just turned fifteen when the original *Star Wars* came out in the summer of 1977, so was basically the perfect target for the film, and for all the mythical and religious imagery and ideas concealed in it. For me, and obviously for millions of other people, that idea of the Force was instantly appealing. George Lucas didn't have to spend much dialogue in the movie getting across what he was talking about, because people just instantly picked up on it. An invisible, universal field that records and unifies everything, everywhere. A force that's all-pervasive, that's sensitive to your thoughts and actions, that records every activity . . . who knows, maybe even your thoughts."

"Well," said Bernie, "I'm more of a *Star Trek* man myself, but I see your point."

"*Star Trek*!" I said. "I could never get with *Star Trek* myself. Spock's too logical."

"Logic is important!" Bernie said.

"Yeah, I know," I said. "But anyhow, whether you're a *Star Trek* or a *Star Wars* man, it just seems to me that that notion of the Force was an incredibly powerful idea. It's one that our minds just say 'Yes' to so immediately that you can't help but wonder if there's a reason for that. By introducing that idea of the Force, *Star Wars* allowed millions of people living in what they thought was a post-religious world to feel, once again, a very potent religious feeling: that they were immersed in an invisible world of some sort, one that they'd known was there all along, and had secretly felt all along, but had just forgotten about on a conscious level. It's an incredibly powerful idea, but it's also, I think, the kind of idea that an awful lot of nonsense could be written about very quickly."

"A lot of nonsense *has* been written about it," said Bernie. "If ever there was a place where Mr. Spock's logical mind is needed, it's in the world of books on the Zero Point Field. And, I'm sorry to say, I've played a part in that, as I've been interviewed by authors who took what I had to say and then twisted it to suit their purposes."

Bernie then, as was his habit, reached behind him and produced one of these books. He was all for my mentioning it by name, but I said that in my experience, calling specific people out didn't really get one anywhere.

"I think it might be best just to sort of turn the other cheek," I said. Then for good measure, I regaled him with several grievances that I'd suffered as a writer, getting ever more worked up as I did so.

"Anyhow," Bernie said, pulling me back on course, "it's a shame that this material gets cheapened like that, because this material is so interesting just as it is, there's no need to overstate any of it. You get pop science or pop spirituality authors writing about it so much that eventually it becomes associated with flaky thinking, with phony science. The Zero Point Field is very precisely, rigorously, and mathematically defined in physics. And its chief characteristic is that it is totally random. All those particles popping into and out of existence do so in a completely wild, chaotic manner. By definition you cannot convey information with them. Most of the new age, fuzzy-wuzzy theories about the Zero Point Field use the extraordinary fact that it's present everywhere to turn it, basically, into, as you say, a kind of equivalent of George Lucas's idea of the Force. The Zero Point Field is an extraordinary phenomenon, but a phenomenon is all it is. It's a part of this world. And as we've covered again and again, God is *not* part of this world. He's above, apart from it, even if in another sense he's deeply immanent in it. Again, if God were just another part of the world, instead of a being categorically above and beyond it, he wouldn't be God."

"Sure," I said. "That's standard theology. Or as you would put it: he created the program, so He's not part of it. God is not a thing-among-things. Not even if that 'thing' is something as crazy and fascinating as the Zero Point Field."

"Right," Bernie said. "But the problem is that when a scientific idea gets popular, it can actually turn out badly for the idea. Crazy as it may sound, if a new scientific idea takes on too much cache in the media, especially the world of fringy writing that tries to slap science and spirituality together in too quick and easy a fashion, the idea can get . . . tainted. Serious researchers get scared to touch it. The subject acquires a stigma, and before you know it, the grant money dries up, the solid research stops, and you don't learn anything more about it. By being so interesting, the subject sinks itself."

"That's ridiculous," I said. "Grant money for an idea shouldn't dry up just because a subject is interesting, for God's sake."

"I couldn't agree more," Bernie said. "But you see, the public images that come from the descriptions and names applied to new scientific discoveries have important ramifications. Look at the Higgs Boson. A boson is a kind of particle, named after an Indian physicist named Satyendra Bose. There are two basic classes of particles: bosons and fermions. All particles can be classified as one or the other of them. So the Higgs Boson is just a particular kind of particle that Higgs and his associates suggested existed. Whether it does exist or not, the excitement around its possible existence has earned it its nickname, the 'God Particle.' And that's a terrible name."

"Right," I said. "Because as soon as you give something a name like that, you not only cheapen the discovery by sensationalizing it, you also do God a disservice by demoting Him down to the physical realm, which is as good as throwing Him in the trash altogether. Traditionally, God is thought to transcend the physical realm completely, but the physical realm reflects His glory all the same. And that means that the more we learn about the world, the more we learn about God, because the world is His handiwork, right? Not that this is a perspective the average scientist would share, I imagine.

"All of this also makes me think of the ancient Greco-Egyptian document known as the Emerald Tablet, where it says: 'As above, so below.' What those words have always meant to me is that while spiritual realities might not, for most of us at least, be directly perceptible, we can gain hints of what the spiritual worlds are like by paying attention to what *this* world is like. But that doesn't mean the two are the same."

I didn't mention this to Bernie at the time, but all of this, it seemed to me, was also illustrated in the way the word "light" appears in the Bible. In the New Testament, especially in the Gospel of John, the state of consciousness Jesus advocates and identifies himself with is constantly compared to light. But the "light" the Prologue to the Gospel of John talks about is clearly not ordinary light—not the light made up of photons that the sun bathes our planet with every day. It's a *higher* light. It's the light God speaks of on the first day of creation when he says: "Let there be light." As is often pointed out, Genesis describes God creating the sun and moon on the fourth day of creation, so the "light" the Bible is talking about on that first day of creation clearly cannot be ordinary physical light. It is, more likely, the same light-that-is-not-light that the Gospel of John talks about when it says:

"In him was life; and the life was the light of men. And the light shineth in darkness; and the darkness comprehended it not."

(Later, when I brought this up with Bernie, he pointed out that in the *Haggadah*, a collection of legends from the tradition of Jewish Kabbalah, it is specifically written: "The light created at the very beginning is not the same as the light emitted by the Sun, the Moon, and stars.")

"As above, so below," I said again to Bernie. "The important thing to remember in discussing the Zero Point Field, it seems to me, is that it can appear to have God-like properties, *but that*

doesn't make it divine. God is God, the physical world is the physical world. But just as humans, being made in God's image, have qualities that can tell us what God is like, so the physical properties of the Zero Point Field have properties that can tell us what God is like as well."

"That also goes," said Bernie, "for what we were talking about the day before yesterday, when I talked about how mathematics 'fits' this universe. You can come up with some extremely abstract mathematical theory, and then later discover that, my God, this fits the laws governing quasars, or galaxy formation."

"So what's the single most important lesson that someone like me, a layman, as they used to say, can learn from this fact that mathematics 'fits' this universe?"

"The lesson," said Bernie, "that we were discussing the other day. That you cannot look at the world around you and take anything for granted, take anything as just 'being there,' with no further discussion of it. Any law of physics that exists has to have come from somewhere. You can't just say, 'Oh, it's a law. It has to be that way.' No it doesn't! When the universe came into being with the Big Bang, some fourteen billion years ago, all kinds of laws were already in place, and the universe went about organizing itself according to those laws. But where did those laws come from? The materialistically based scientists who believe in the Big Bang have no trouble accepting that these laws existed. They have to, because without a law, physical matter doesn't know what to do with itself. Indeed, without a plethora of laws, it can't exist to begin with.

> *"Any law of physics that exists has to have come from somewhere."*

"But the important thing is that a lot of those laws didn't have to be 'set' at exactly the setting they have. In principle—and everyone agrees on this—they could have been set any old way at all. If any of the laws that were in place when our universe came into being—any single one of them at all—were set differently, then our universe would either be profoundly different from the way it is, or it wouldn't exist at all, because the Big Bang would have been nothing more than a big blip, with the universe coming into being, and popping back out of it, instantly.

"Imagine the universe is like an oven. The knobs could be turned up to high, down to low, or anywhere in between. But the thing about our universe is that the settings for at least half a dozen constants were tuned so finely that the precision of it boggles the imagination.

"Take," Bernie continued, "the gravitational constant, the 'setting' that gravity is set at. Gravity, as you know, is yet another of those many aspects of our life that we largely take for granted.

We are all so used to gravity that we tend not to give it much thought, but that's just because we're used to it. After all, it's been around as long as we have, so it's easy to ignore it—as people in fact did for thousands of years before Newton drew our attention to its existence.

"Why does the earth attract objects to itself, so that if you climb a ladder and step off, you risk breaking your leg? Because, of course, of the force of gravity. But gravity does not need to be set at the specific setting it is in fact set at. It could be stronger (you'd break both legs falling off that ladder, and have a harder time climbing up it as well), or weaker (once you got to the top of that ladder, you could step off and drift slowly back down to earth). We understand how gravity is stronger or weaker on different planets, because of the different size of those planets. But that's not what we're talking about here. We're talking about a 'setting' that takes place before all that—a setting that defines exactly how strong the force of gravity is going to be that precedes the coming into existence of matter itself. A setting that was set at the very dawn of the universe.

"So . . . the common assumption is that the gravitational force just is what it is, and that's the end of it. It could have been no different. But this is far from the case. Gravity in our universe has been set at a certain strength, and it has been set *very* precisely. We use mathematics to understand how God created the cosmos, because *mathematics is the language this cosmos speaks*. So if you want to understand God in our universe, you need to understand mathematics, because God is one hell of a mathematician."

> *"We use mathematics to understand how God created the cosmos, because mathematics is the language this cosmos speaks."*

CHAPTER 13

One Very Nice Blueberry Pie

IMAGINE WALKING INTO your house after work and finding a pie on the counter. It's warm, but not too hot to eat. You cut a slice of it, and discover that it's a blueberry pie, one of your favorites. The crust is perfect—not too flaky, not too dense. The filling is equally masterful—not too runny, not too solid. It's one incredible blueberry pie.

How did this pie come about? Did it just happen to appear on the counter of your kitchen? And if it did, what accounts for its singularly excellent quality? For it being, in fact, the best pie you ever tasted? If it had been baked just a little longer, the crust, now just right, would be burned. A little less, and it would be too doughy. On top of that, someone took it out of the oven just in time for it to be the perfect temperature for eating when you arrived home.

This, in essence, was the point Bernie was making to me

now about the universe. It was a point I had had a little experience with already. During my nine years of work at *Guideposts* magazine, I'd had a chance to interview Lee Strobel, the former *Chicago Tribune* reporter who started out as a vigorous nonbeliever but who, after following his wife into Christianity, produced a score of books giving the case in favor of such things as Christ, faith, and—my favorite—his 2004 book, *The Case for a Creator*.

Our universe isn't just nicely put together. It is very nicely put together. So much so that it has become extremely difficult for scientists—or anyone else—to argue that it just happened to come into existence in the way it has without any design or purpose acting on its behalf.

Strobel's *The Case for a Creator*, and the interview I ended up conducting with him for the magazine after reading it, gave me my introduction to what Bernie was now talking to me about— to the fact that in the course of the last few decades, our universe has revealed itself to be a whole lot more like that blueberry pie than anyone had ever before imagined. Our universe isn't just nicely put together. It is *very* nicely put together. So much so that it has become extremely difficult for scientists—or anyone else—to argue that it just happened to come into existence in the way it has without any design or purpose acting on its be-half. In short, it has become very hard to argue that there wasn't something—or some *One*—behind it.

Our universe, as Bernie argues at length in *The Purpose-Guided Universe*, is Purposeful with a capital "P." Nature is brimming with things that function awfully, awfully well. We are so used to seeing purpose at work in the world around us, so used to seeing things just where they're supposed to be, *and so used to being told that there is nothing remarkable about this*, that we take this purposefulness we encounter in the world around us all but completely for granted, despite the deep damage that this attitude does to us on the inside. For on the inside, we quite simply know it is wrong.

We are so used to seeing purpose at work in the world around us, so used to seeing things just where they're supposed to be, and so used to being told that there is nothing remarkable about this, that we take this purposefulness we encounter in the world around us all but completely for granted, despite the deep damage that this attitude does to us on the inside. For on the inside, we quite simply know it is wrong.

The awesome efficiency of the natural world is a kind of given in the modern world, and the explanation for its marvelous beauty and efficiency is simple. Life, we are told, evolved randomly, and over time the organisms that were best at surviving were the most likely to breed, and so to transfer their marvelously, but meaninglessly, efficient genes on to their young. There's no real reason for it, other than that once life evolved, it was somehow blindly but relentlessly "driven" to keep evolving. Simple, really.

Thirty years or so ago, scientists discovered that just about everything about the basic structure of the universe is balanced on a razor's edge for life to exist. The coincidences are far too significant to attribute this to mere chance or to claim that it needs no explanation. The dials are set too precisely to have been a random accident. Most scientists refuse to acknowledge that there is anything strange about these extraordinarily precise settings. And the reason they do so is clear: These fantastically precise settings suggest the two ideas materialist science is most set on denying: that God exists, and that He built the universe with a purpose in mind.

As I discovered that day on the football field back in my elementary school days, humans are creatures of purpose. It's just built into us. We are creatures who are not comfortable unless we feel like we are going somewhere. *Telos* means "purpose" in Greek, and in the ancient world, particularly with the Greeks (and among those Greeks, particularly with Aristotle), it was assumed that everything in life had its *telos* or (another Greek word) its *entelechy*, its reason for being.

"Purpose" can have two different senses. Its deeper meaning is the philosophical one: the one that we conjure up when we ask, "Does life have any purpose?"

The more boring one is, obviously, what we mean when we ask, say, "What's the purpose of a toothbrush?" In this case, "purpose" is essentially another word for "function."

Yet though they differ, these two senses of the word are closely connected. For only in a world where purpose with a capital "P" is possible can there be objects possessing purpose with a small "p."

Only in a world where purpose with a capital "P" is possible can there be objects possessing purpose with a small "p."

CHAPTER 14

Purpose

THE COSMIC STORY I was given as a schoolchild (in science class, after the morning business of the Lord's Prayer was over) was one in which things just sort of happened, and kept on just sort of happening, in a bored, random sort of way, for vast amounts of time, until, finally, after an immeasurably long period of random, run-of-the-mill events, humans evolved and built civilization.

The story ran something like this: The universe just happened to explode into being some fourteen billion years ago with the Big Bang, which just happened to occur because of a random quantum fluctuation which set into place a series of laws, which arose spontaneously, and just happened to be the exactly right laws for our universe to develop.

The hydrogen atoms[1] that blasted out after being formed in the first seconds after the Big Bang occurred just happened to form into stars, where, after millions of years, through the process of fusion, the hydrogen atoms at the heart of those first stars were converted into helium atoms.

Hydrogen atoms have one proton in their nucleus. Four (altogether) hydrogen atoms can be combined to make one helium atom, which, accordingly, has two protons and two neutrons. In the course of this transformation from four hydrogen atoms into one helium atom, a small amount of matter is turned into energy. Matter and energy are, as Bernie and I covered, the same thing, and as Einstein's equation $E = mc^2$ demonstrates, a little bit of matter transforms into a whole lot of energy. It was this energy that made the first ancient stars shine in the night skies of the early universe.

When one of these early stars turned all or most of its hydrogen atoms into helium, the drop in energy production at its heart caused the star to collapse. All those helium atoms rushing into the star's dying center turned what was previously a huge, gaseous star into an intensely small, dense one. The force of all that suddenly created density, and the jump in gravitational force that resulted from it, started the process of fusion (the squishing of two atoms together into a single, larger atom) anew, with all those helium atoms cramming together to form atoms with even larger atomic numbers— that is, atoms with more protons (and neutrons) in their nuclei.

---

1 All atoms at this stage of the universe are really only the nuclei of the atoms because the electrons are ionized away.

In short, the once large and steady star turned into an ongoing fusion-powered nuclear bomb, which—after creating some of the atoms on the periodic table with more protons at their center, like the ones in your body right now, all of which were forged in the heart of ancient, now-dead stars—exploded, sending those new, more complex atoms out into the universe, providing the raw material for other stars to form.

Gradually, over the course of billions of years, the intense mashing together of atoms at the heart of these ancient stars slowly but surely produced every element in the periodic table.

One of the more complex atoms created by this process was carbon. Carbon is the building block of organic life. No life would exist on earth without it, and scientists have come up with no element, real or imagined, that could do the job carbon does in supporting life with the same kind of dazzling efficiency. On every level, carbon seems to have been custom-made to serve as the primary building block of organic life.

> *One of the more complex atoms created by this process was carbon. Carbon is the building block of organic life. No life would exist on earth without it, and scientists have come up with no element, real or imagined, that could do the job carbon does in supporting life with the same kind of dazzling efficiency.*

Carbon, however, would be much less plentiful in the universe were it not for a process (first proposed by British astronomer Sir Fred Hoyle) in which a carbon atom, when it forms in a star's blistering white heart, tends to encourage the other atoms around it to follow suit, basically turning those stars into extremely efficient carbon factories. A very lucky turn of events, for with no other element does this phenomenon occur. It is absolutely unique to carbon. Millions of years before carbon-based life first arose on earth, we were already on a really, really remarkable winning streak.

Earth, along with the other seven (sorry, Pluto) planets in our solar system, formed gradually from passing stray bits of matter that entered the sun's orbit in response to its gravitational pull. Earth happened to end up with an especially generous supply of complex elements, most especially those—like nitrogen, hydrogen, and of course carbon—that are most essential for organic life.

Earth also just happened to be given a large supply of iron, which settled into place at the earth's core, where, thanks to the heat generated by the intense gravitational pressure at the earth's center, it remained (and continues to remain) in a molten state. It was thus able to send out heat that kept the earth's crust warm and malleable, allowing for continental formation and drift. This gave us a planet with land and water, rather than just water, water, everywhere.

On the subject of water: It should also be mentioned that it just happens to be the only molecule that floats when in a solid state, a very convenient state of affairs when one considers what our earth would be like if ice sank. (Hint: once again, no land since oceans would freeze from the bottom up. And, as Bernie added: "strange-looking drinks.")

But to get back to us, and how we happened to arise just here, on this chance planet in this chance universe. Somehow or other, the soup of organic molecules and elements floating about in the earth's seas about four billion years ago eventually (and actually rather quickly) managed to arrange themselves into living matter. How? Well, if we listen to the dominant scientific narrative today, they just sort of did.

Back in the early seventies, when I was in elementary school, the image we were given was of a sort of primordial stew of elements, splashing about in the earth's first seas. Over tremendous lengths of time, these atoms and molecules banged together again and again, until finally, somewhere, at some particular point (and maybe with the help of a fortuitous lightning strike), those molecules fell together in such a way as to form amino acids—the building blocks of proteins, and of deoxyribonucleic acid, or DNA. DNA is the compound which, as everyone knows, carries the information that allows cells to construct other cells and deliver the specific information needed by those cells to reproduce. Cellular walls just sort of happened to form around these primitive strands of DNA, and voilà, the first true cells were formed.

The most primitive cell is more complex by far than any computer humans have yet constructed, so it is quite a bit of a coincidence that such an entity should have formed for no rhyme or reason amid the jostling primordial soup filling the earth's first oceans. But so, regardless, the story goes. And with initial cell formation out of the way, it was only a matter of time (lots and lots more of it) before those cells banded together to create multicellular organisms, which then (what else could they do?) turned into larger, and ever more sophisticated, sea creatures, which evolved by the mechanism of natural selection as they competed for food, first in the sea, and then (why not?) on land.

All of this may seem quite unlikely—and indeed it is preposterously so, in every aspect. Evolution surely plays a major role in the development of life on earth. "But," as Bernie told me, "the detailed requirements are so enormous that some degree of skepticism is warranted: especially for day one when the first microscopic organism amazingly finds itself alive.

"The late scientist Stephen J. Gould, a world-renowned expert on evolution, pointed out major discrepancies between standard Darwinian theory and fossil records. He claimed to see 'punctuated equilibrium' (Gould's wording) rather than gradual evolution.

"But as materialist science will remind you, should you find yourself getting too excited about any of it, you should remember that there exists a pair of related, and each perfectly good, explanations for all of this, and which, conveniently, remove all wonder and mystery from the world as we find it. The first of these is the Multiverse Theory and the other is the Many Worlds Theory.

Bernie was quick to tell me that he was not keen on either of them. Good scientist that he is, Bernie is pretty even-minded about whether his and his colleagues' theory about the Zero Point Field may someday turn out to be correct. To Bernie's mind, it's either the Zero Point Field that creates the inertial drag on subatomic particles that gives rise to our apparently solid universe, or it's the Higgs Field. Whichever way it eventually turns out will be fine with him.

Not so with the Multiverse and Many Worlds theories. He is genuinely aghast at these, and it soon became easy for me to understand why.

Our universe is too remarkable,
too dazzling in the intelligence it
evidences in its every aspect, to have
come into being just by chance.

To begin with the earlier, and simpler, Multiverse Theory: It suggests that there is not just one universe, but many. Our universe is but one among perhaps countless others.

We have no way of knowing whether these universes actually exist, because, being *other* universes, they're completely separate from our own. But they might be out there (who knows?), and if they are, they do us the tremendous service of allowing us to look upon our own universe as nothing special, as having arisen purely by chance and accident, and having been put together by nothing and nobody.

Our universe is too remarkable, too dazzling in the intelligence it evidences in its every aspect, to have come into being just by chance. A great many all-but-impossibly-unlikely factors led to its being the place it is, and us being the beings we are. *Unless* ... there is a virtually unlimited number of other, subpar universes out there, in which case all is well again.

For a single universe (given the vast amount of evidence from every scientific discipline, from physics to astronomy to biology to geology) points to a creator who created it with purpose and intelligence. And once you let those two beasts (purpose and intelligence) in the door, you have no choice but to grant at least possible existence to that disaster of all disasters: God.

In these other universes, the Multiverse Theory says, all sorts of different laws and processes are at work. What kind? We have no idea. These universes may all be different from each other and operate under different physical laws, though they were all probably born when ours was. But the important thing is that because these universes *might* exist, we have an explanation of why it is that our universe (mistakenly) appears so designed, in so many countless ways, to support life—specifically human life. All sorts of unlikely things have happened in our universe, because our universe is the one, among all those countless others, where all these strings of mind-bogglingly lucky breaks just happened to have occurred. Out of billions or trillions of universes, we ended up, or grew up, in the only one where the dice were rolled and came up double-sixes . . . more than a trillion trillion trillion trillion times in a row.

So . . . rather than acknowledging that the more we learn, the clearer it becomes that Someone was behind the design of our universe, this theory suggests that our universe only *seems* remarkable because it just happens to be the one universe, among all the vast, endless legions of universes out there, where such marvels have taken place. Again: We can't detect those other universes. There is absolutely no evidence for them whatsoever. But if we could see them, we'd no doubt find that most, or all, of them contain no life. Or, for that matter, anything else that smacks of order, purpose, or meaning. All those qualities are flukes: flukes that happen to have shown up—one after another, and another, and another—in our universe alone.

Out of billions or trillions of universes, we ended up, or grew up, in the only one where the dice were rolled and came up double-sixes . . . more than a trillion trillion trillion trillion times in a row.

Of course, it would be very convenient if we *could* catch a glimpse of all those half-baked, lifeless, poorly made universes, because then we could really and truly *know* what materialist science so confidently preaches to us: that our universe, remarkable as it seems to the naïve observer, really isn't remarkable at all.

But we can't. And, according to Bernie, we never will.

"By definition," he told me, "another universe is . . . *another universe*. It operates by different laws. And because we are creatures of *this* universe, with our bodies and minds created according to its laws and not those of another universe, there is simply no way to find out if any of those hypothetical other universes exist."

"Of course," Bernie told me, "If God made one universe he can surely make many; in for a penny, in for a pound, as the British like to say. The Multiverse Theory can be formulated with or without a creator, but it's certainly true that its raison d'être is to explain away all the many signs that our universe is special.

"It is also interesting that the most popular physics theories involving universes find that other dimensions are required by the string-theory and M-theory concepts.

"If the Multiverse Theory is not your cup of tea and you are still anxious to be comforted that you live in a pointless, Godless, thoroughly purpose-free universe, there exists another theory to help you out. This is the Many Worlds Theory proposed by Hugh Everett in 1957. It suggests not that a vast number of universes were born when our own was, but that new universes are born *every time a subatomic reaction* (that is, an interaction among particles, the ultimate building blocks of all matter) *takes place*.

"And these universes are not just born because of particle physics," Bernie told me. "You play a role in creating new universes every day, as does every other human being and animal on the planet.

"Say," continued Bernie, "you are deciding between cereal and eggs for breakfast. This momentous decision would create a universe where you eat cereal and a universe where you eat eggs. But it gets worse. Each of these two universes creates multiple other universes, such as an eggs-with-sausage universe and a universe where you choose eggs and bacon. Let's not forget the gluten-free pancakes. Every decision you make births a new universe. In other words, thousands, or more like trillions, of new universes were born in the time it took me to tell you this. The splitting off of new universes is endless.

"Let's look," said Bernie, "at another example of what this would mean. Yogi Berra once said, 'If you see a fork in the road, take it.' Say someone is driving along and comes to a fork in the road. Well, according to the Many Worlds Theory, he could really take Yogi's advice—that is, one of him would take the left fork, while another 'him' would take a right. In other words, the choice of taking the left or the right fork creates a duplicate of the person. But in fact, what's created is not just a duplicate of that person. What's created is a duplicate of the entire universe, so that there's one for the driver who turned left, and another for the driver who turned right. We cannot, of course, see this other parallel universe, or the trillions of others that are arising all the time, but the choice faced by the driver, and the fact that both options were open to him, necessitated its creation.

"But it's not just human choice that creates these splits, and the new universes that pop into being to accommodate them. Your cat deciding to jump down off one side of the bed instead of the other will split the universe too."

"And," I said, "the evidence of all these constantly multiplying universes . . . "

"Is zilch," Bernie said. "There's no evidence whatsoever."

"Well," I said. "I get it. I mean, I get the idea. But I don't get why you're so worked up about it. I mean, the idea is obviously idiotic."

"It may sound that way to you," said Bernie. "But it's accepted by an extraordinarily large number of respected scientists as the best explanation for why our universe is the way it is."

Bernie searched around on his desk and came up with the January 25, 2017, issue of *New Scientist*.

"This is from an article—a favorable one—on the Many Worlds Theory. 'Some of your doppelgangers,' it says, 'mimic your every thought and action, only with a snazzier haircut. Some live in a world where the Nazis won the Second World War, or where the dinosaurs survived, or where things fall up instead of down. Not here, not in this universe. But they are out there—in the multiverse, where every possible world exists, along with all the infinite versions of you.'

"To me this is not just insanity. It's a free country. Everyone's entitled to their opinion, even if, to me at least, that opinion is nuts. What's troubling to me is the profound moral relativism that is built into this theory. The idea of infinite versions of your-self is not only abhorrent to the intellect, it is immoral. If physics can turn you into an infinite number of copies of yourself, what is the point of living a virtuous life? It removes all the dignity I have as a human being. If there are a million, or a trillion, or a trillion trillion trillion other Bernie Haisches out there, and more appearing every moment, I lose all my standing as a single, conse-quential individual. The theory is, then, not only highly unlikely (again, there is not a shred of evidence for it), but . . . evil."

"So how come," I asked, "Hugh Everett felt it necessary to come up with this theory? I mean, the Multiverse Theory, if you can persuade yourself to believe in it, is enough to allow one to dis-miss the apparent intelligence and purpose at work in our world. Why another theory, especially one that's so much *more* unlikely?"

"Because," said Bernie, "the real target of the Many Worlds Theory is not the apparent intelligence with which our uni-verse was made, but something trickier, and more dangerous. It was introduced as a solution to the conundrum of how the consciousness of experimenters seemed to affect the outcome of certain quantum experiments.

"At its most primary level," Bernie continued, "light is com-posed of particles called photons. A photon can manifest as a wave or a particle and will do either one or the other, depending on how scientists choose to measure it.

"That's weird, but it's still manageable. What's *not* manage-able is that if an experiment is performed in a sealed box, and a photon is made to behave in a certain way, and the experiment is done, and the photon has done whatever it's going to do . . .

"Well, here's where the problem lies. Inside the box, the experiment is *over*. It's a done deal. Inside, the photon has made the choice to either behave like a wave or behave like a particle. It's done, it's finished, it's irreversible. The photon has done either the one or the other. It has happened.

"But the scientists who have performed this experiment now have a choice. They can open the box and measure the outcome in such a way that they treat the photon as a particle, or they can open it and treat the photon as a wave. Again, just for good measure, let's reiterate. The experiment is over, and inside the box, the photon has made its choice."

("Choice," by the way, isn't really the right word to use here, because, as Bernie told me on several occasions, "particles don't know anything." The particles are operating according to the instructions of the "program" of the universe, which God designed, but which He is outside of.)

"It's a done deal," Bernie continued. "Whatever has happened inside the box has *happened*, period. But when the experimenters open the box and make their choice of how to measure the outcome, the photon particle in the box will accommodate their choice, even though it had no way of 'knowing' how they would choose to measure it."

"And that fact—the fact that subatomic phenomena react according to how we choose to think about them—is so dangerous that the Many Worlds Theory had to be devised to combat it?"

"Yes."

"Why?"

"Because otherwise, if you don't have the Many Worlds Theory to neutralize every subatomic experiment in which human consciousness plays a part . . ."

"You are forced," I said, "to take consciousness seriously. As real. As real as . . ."

"As real," said Bernie, "as the material world. In fact, as more real. And that is something scientists were not, and are not, prepared to do."

The mind is a real thing. Descartes's division of the world into *res cogitans* and *res extensa*, the (unreal) world inside our heads and the (real) world outside it, led to a world where only physical things are real. That's the world both Bernie and I grew up in. But that world is part of the past. For it is not the material world that is real, but the mind. We are not passing phantoms, moving through a world of objects that are real and more lasting than us. Instead, exactly the opposite is the case.

"On the most fundamental level," Bernie told me, "only consciousness exists."

CHAPTER 15

Burning Man

LIFE AT THE Haisch residence, I was discovering, was a busy one, due chiefly to Marsha's schedule rather than Bernie's. A native Californian, she was raised in Burbank and comes from a long line of musicians. Her grandmother was a music teacher and concert pianist in Ruston, Louisiana. She taught Marsha's dad, Rankin Sims, to play the piano, and though very talented ("He could play anything by ear," Marsha told me), he elected to become an aeronautical space engineer and moved to the Los Angeles area to work at the Lockheed Skunk Works. It was there that he met Marsha's mother. Later the family moved to Sunnyvale so her dad could work at Lockheed Missiles and Space, where he played a part in engineering some of the Mariner missions to Mars.

Marsha first sang onstage when she was three. "We were eating at a supper club in Scottsdale, Arizona, with some friends," she told me. "I walked up onstage to ask the pianist if he would please play 'Let Me Call You Sweetheart' and he said, 'Only if you will sing it.' So I did."

Marsha got her bachelor's degree in Music and Teaching credential at the University of California, Santa Barbara, and her master's in Music at Notre Dame de Namur University in Belmont, California, and taught music until the school where she taught closed down. Needing a job, she sought her dad's help and got one at Lockheed Palo Alto Research Laboratory.

"Because I was a pianist," she told me, "I could type really fast."

It was also at Lockheed that Marsha got her training in keeping absentminded scientists in line.

"I helped to keep the scientists organized. That whole cliché about scientists having their heads in the clouds most of the time is pretty much true."

Marsha did administrative work for the gaggle of geniuses in her charge, prepared their papers for publication, helped organize their trips to meetings and conventions, and was in charge of the coffee club as well.

"So you liked the work?" I asked.

"Oh yes," she said. "The truth is, I always thought nerds were cute."

It was at Lockheed that Marsha met Bernie, who at first was just another Brainiac with challenged life skills.

"I'd known Bernie for about three years, when one morning we ran into each other at the copy machine. I asked Bernie how he was. He said, like a little boy whose dog had just died, 'Terrible. It looks like my wife and I are going to get a divorce.'

"'Wow,' I said. 'My husband just asked *me* for a divorce.' Bernie suggested we go to lunch and talk about it. By this time I'd taken a real liking to the physicists I worked with. It was interesting to me the way these guys were almost crippled by their extreme intelligence. As nerdy as most of them were, there was something a little romantic to me about them. They were just so . . . *other*. So maybe it's no surprise that Bernie and I hit it off. A year and a half later, we got married."

The Haisches got going on a classic *Brady Bunch*–style mixed-marriage family. "I have a daughter, Elizabeth, from a previous marriage, and Bernie has his two kids, Katherine and Taylor, whose room you're in. I've been a mom to his kids since they were four and six years old, and we're good friends with Bernie's ex, Pamela. We celebrate most holidays together."

Bernie and Marsha's marriage was, from the start, a collaborative one on all fronts. Marsha helped Bernie run the *Journal of Scientific Exploration*, serving as the magazine's executive editor during his ten years as editor in chief. Bernie also shares Marsha's love of music, and together they've written about a hundred songs, and produced many of them at the recording studio they built into the second floor of the house we were in, where Marsha gave her daily string of music lessons. One of their songs,

"Common Ground," got a little airplay on country-and-western stations in the early nineties.

Marsha is, in short, just the kind of big colorful ball of energy and activity that a reclusive astrophysicist needs around to keep him firmly anchored in the daily world.

"Bernie really is the absentminded professor," I said to Marsha one day. "I mean, he's right out of central casting. He makes me feel like I'm *not* absentminded. And that takes a lot."

"Yeah he is," Marsha said in her upbeat, matter-of-fact way. "You know," she continued, "that reminds me of something I wanted to ask you. Burning Man is happening out in the desert next week. I didn't think I'd be able to make it this year because I waited too long to rent a camper, and now they're all gone. But just today I got a line on a rental for a good price, and I'd really like to go."

"*Burning Man?*" I said. "You're going to rent a camper and drive to *Burning Man?*"

It turned out my suspicions about Marsha's hippie past had been right on the mark. Burning Man is a yearly festival that attracts about seventy thousand participants to the middle of a vast, treeless stretch of Nevada that's as flat and hot as a giant frying pan. Depending on whom you talk to, it is a cosmically charged gathering of positive people living at the edge of the new paradigm, people out to change the world into a new and better place . . . or a makeshift assemblage of sixties casualties, misfits, show-offs, and druggies.

My suspicion was that it was a mixture of both, and while I had nothing against the event, I would have gladly submitted to fifteen or so minutes of water-boarding rather than attend myself. But . . . if Marsha wanted to go, that was fine with me.

"Anyhow," Marsha said, "I was wondering if you'd stay here and take care of Bernie while I'm away. If I'm not here to make him take his medication"—she shot a look at Bernie, who was listening to all this like a dog that didn't understand people language—"he won't take it."

Bernie suddenly seemed to snap to attention.

"Don't be ridiculous," he said. "Of course I'll take my medication."

"I don't know," I said to Bernie. "I've been watching you these past days, and I kind of think Marsha's right. You *are* pretty absentminded. Anyhow, I'd love to stay. We can pack in a bunch more interviews before I head back."

Back where? I thought to myself, even as I said this. I had no real plans of where I would stay when I returned to the East Coast. As welcoming as Bernie and Marsha had been, I certainly didn't feel like I belonged at their house, tucked into that little room with the piano and those Three Stooges videos, for too much longer.

But there was, I had come to notice more and more, something really curious that happened, to both Bernie and me, when we sat down to have our talks. Something in the air changed, and as Bernie tried to lay out for me just why he was so excited about the vision of the world he was now living in, I would catch some of that spirit, and find—at least for the length of the talk—that I didn't really care that I had no real home to speak of, and no solid plans on what I was going to do next.

"Solidity"—the word and, more importantly, a new understanding of the very concept itself, was beginning to take me over. Sometimes, staring over at the tranquil, dignified stone figure of the Japanese Lucky Cat that I had set up in my room at the Haisches' right next to Bernie's box of Stooge videos, I would feel, deep inside me, a funny new sense of *presence*. With my possessions, my finances, my future . . . with *everything* in my life in total disarray, I was coming into contact with a sense of what I could only call *anchored*-ness. My moods could be good or they could be bad. I could be—for no particular reason—in a cheery mood, or sunk in in a black, miserable, *how-soon-can-I-take-my-Ambien* funk. But regardless, below and beyond these surface conditions, there was a strange yet undeniable undercurrent at work: I was beginning to experience my existence in a way I never had before, and I intended to talk to Bernie a little longer so that I could figure out just what this feeling was, and how I could perhaps develop it further.

One thing was for sure. "Consciousness," one of the most brutally overused and misunderstood words around, was recovering a strange, original freshness for me. In particular, I was starting to see how this word, which did not exist at the time the Gospels were written, brought those texts to life for me in strange and exciting new ways.

Jesus spoke in the Gospel of Matthew of the pearl of great price, and he suggested that this pearl was strangely available to all, and was, in fact, already in our possession. This idea, beloved and familiar as it was, took on a curious new resonance as my talks with Bernie continued. Perhaps because I now knew that the entire world was composed solely of consciousness, I felt a curious reversal in how I felt about my inner world and the outer world around me. Consciousness was real, while the outer world of solid objects that surrounded me each day was not. I somehow felt, somehow *knew*, that this was true, and this knowledge had implications that spread into how I actually experienced myself in the world.

CHAPTER 16

Bachelors

I TOLD MARSHA I'D be happy to watch over Bernie, even if, as Bernie said, he didn't need any watching over. I also said I wanted to head back down to LA for a couple of days before doing so. I'd now been a guest at the Haisches' for close to a week, and though it was all comfortable and friendly, there was something about Bernie's and my daily talks that not only nourished but also drained me. Taking a week away would let me clear my head and come back ready to finish up my interviews and, hopefully, find that third Key.

I got back up to Redwood City the afternoon after Marsha's departure. She'd been a little upset when I told her Bernie would have to stay alone for a night, but I found Bernie no worse for wear for having been alone a full twenty-four hours.

"I see you didn't burn the house down," I said, letting myself in the front door and spotting Bernie on the couch.

"No," Bernie said. "House is still standing. So . . . shall we do an hour or so of taping tonight?"

"Tonight?" I said with surprise. It was around seven, I was worn out and stale from the drive, and the last thing I felt ready for was a plunge into particle physics. I begged off, telling Bernie we had seven empty days ahead of us—surely enough for him to get any and everything else off his chest that he felt he needed to.

A tad reluctantly, Bernie accepted. Around eight o'clock I left him to his CNN in the den, and holed up, once again, in Taylor's room. Back in LA I had cut back my Ambien to the usual one a night, but now I took two again, and was out by nine.

"You wouldn't catch me dead at Burning Man," I said to Bernie the next morning, as he sat at the dining table reading the hard copy of the *San Francisco Chronicle* that washed up, somewhat anachronistically to my mind, on his driveway each morning.

"Me neither," said Bernie. "But Marsha . . . she's been going for a couple of years now and she's become sort of a mother figure to some of the kids there. She loves it."

I told Bernie I'd be ready to have our first talk of the day shortly.

"I was thinking," I said, pointing to the big, brown, L-shaped couch in their sunken, totally seventies-style living room, "that maybe with Marsha not teaching her students, we could branch out a little and do our talks in there."

"Sure," Bernie said. "Don't see why not."

I have always worked best in the morning, and late midday has always been a struggle for me. Bernie seemed to suffer from the same ailment. During those days when Marsha was absent, both of us would be pretty much at loose ends except for when my phone was on and we were talking physics and so forth. Then that odd atmosphere would descend. The objects in the room would become somehow . . . *different*, and I would once again start to feel, at moments, like I was what Bernie said I was: a real being, living amid a world of virtual objects; a being who was more—much more—than met the eye.

As Bernie slowly but surely continued to win me over to his vision of the world, I got into the habit, when going for a walk or the gym or to a bookstore or to whatever fast-food restaurant I'd chosen to get Bernie and me our dinner at that night, of trying to really *feel* the facts of what Bernie had been telling me: that I was not an ephemeral bit of nothing passing through a world of solid lasting objects, but just the opposite: a being whose physical body was made, literally, of atoms cooked in the heart of ancient stars, who had been raised with great care by my local star, the sun that blazed a mere ninety-two million miles above us, and whose mind and heart had been created, mindfully and purposefully and with an expertise beyond all comprehension, by God.

I immediately noticed that conducting our talks out of Bernie's study had a kind of liberating effect on us both. I felt like, with two Keys out of the way and (I had somehow decided) only one left, I was ready to tackle some more daring topics, to take things a little farther afield.

> *I was not an ephemeral bit of nothing passing through a world of solid lasting objects, but just the opposite: a being whose physical body was made, literally, of atoms cooked in the heart of ancient stars, who had been raised with great care by my local star . . . and whose mind and heart were created, mindfully and purposefully . . . by God.*

"So Bernie," I said that first morning of our solo week, "it seems to me that the most important thing I've come away with from these talks so far is an appreciation of consciousness—of what it really means, and of how little our culture values it today.

"It also seems to me that this knowledge means I should do something about it—but I'm still not really sure what. But . . . I do believe that all of this has something to do with the idea that faith is active, not passive. The New Testament sentence that seems to me of greatest importance in this regard is John 5:8, where Jesus tells the stricken man to rise.

"Some translations use the more colloquial 'Get up,' and to me, that two-word command contains the essence of everything we need to do in a world that scientists try to tell us is cold and pointless. Faith-wise these days, it seems like the world is trying extra hard to knock us down, and to knock us down again the minute we struggle to our feet. And yet, the Gospel texts suggest, if the world has knocked us down, there is always a hand there, ready to reach out and pull us up. Faith, through being active, and incorporating the intellect rather than pushing it aside, suggests that truly unknown possibilities lie ahead for all of us.

"As our talks have underlined for me already, genuine faith is, if anything, easier now than it was before the advent of modern science, and the more we know of that science, the easier our faith becomes. Even when things seem terrible, it is always possible, faith-wise, *to get up.* And far from holding us back, science is today's version of that hand reaching out to help us. In a way, I see it almost as a challenge, as if we are being dared to see the real bounty we are being offered today, in terms of knowledge of our world and our place in it. Even as, at the same time, a chorus of voices is telling us just the opposite—that that we have no hope for any deeper understanding of God, or of ourselves."

"Absolutely," said Bernie. "Science is just exactly that helping hand, even though, most of the time, it's presented as being just the opposite. Listen to this," he said, getting slowly to his feet and heading off to his office.

In a moment he came back with a book—one which I recognized easily enough: Stephen Hawking's *Brief History of Time*.

"Stephen Hawking," said Bernie, "is probably the single most revered scientist alive today. People hang on his every word—not just about science, but, more importantly, about what science means. What, in short, the point of it all is. 'I believe,' he says here, 'the simplest explanation is, there is no God. No one created the universe and no one directs our fate. This leads me to a profound realization that there probably is no heaven and no afterlife either. We have this one life to appreciate the grand design of the universe and for that, I am extremely grateful.'

"I admire Hawking," Bernie said. "His achievements, both as a physicist and as a human being coping with overwhelming challenges, are impossible to dispute. But reading a statement like that, I can't help but ask what, exactly, there is to be so grateful for?"

"Oh, yeah," I said. "Totally." I picked up my iPhone and, while leaving the "record" function running, rummaged around on the Internet for a quote from Steven Weinberg:

"Listen to this," I said to Bernie. " 'The effort to understand the universe is one of the very few things that lifts human life a little above the level of farce, and gives it some of the grace of tragedy.' That quote is just about as famous as that one from Hawking you just read me. But *listen* to it. Basically, human beings have the option, if they work really hard and are very talented, to raise themselves an inch or so above the sick, wretched joke that is the universe. At least for a moment or two. But what is the highest level of achievement, of insight, of getting to the real truth of what the universe is about, that is available to us? The grace of tragedy! That just kills me."

"I know what you mean," said Bernie, as if seeing my bid and raising me. "I was watching a rerun of Carl Sagan's *Cosmos* recently. In it, Sagan talked about the wonder of the universe, how extraordinary it all is, and how lucky we are to be living at a time when we can see all this wonder . . . for a brief, flashing moment. Sagan's tone was upbeat, he was all good intentions. But to me his remarks completely echoed Hawking's and Weinberg's. For these men, these enormously accomplished and passionate scientists, the most inspired and exciting vision of the universe available to us—is . . . completely hopeless, completely grim."

"Yeah," I said. "Totally. Like, I'm a crummy little ant of a tourist, getting a quick peek at all this vast, impersonal magnificence that just happens, through millions of years of blind natural selection, to have spat me out for no reason. I'm an accidental being, accidentally conscious, and doomed almost immediately to enter back into the darkness. I look around, with my accidentally produced mind and my accidentally produced senses, at this magnificence that has close to nothing to do with me, and I'm supposed to emit a quick little '*cheep-cheep*' of wonder before I'm smashed back into oblivion.

PROOF OF GOD

"That reminds me of a line from an essay by the novelist Jonathan Franzen that I read recently. It was just a throwaway line in a piece of his, but it stopped me in my tracks. 'I have a brief tenure on earth,' Franzen said, 'bracketed by infinities of nothingness.' What a statement! I mean, Franzen is a smart guy, and his word is gospel in the literary world. And yet . . . he's capable of a statement like that. A statement that is almost adolescent in its gloom, but which is also so simply . . . wrong. And, I mean"—I paused and took a swig from the can of Red Bull that was on the table in front of us—"who *cares* how many stars there are in the universe, or how cool it must look when a supernova explodes, if you yourself aren't a part of it, if you aren't involved in the story in some deeper, longer, more significant way?

> *"Who* cares *how many stars there are in the universe, or how cool it must look when a supernova explodes, if you yourself aren't a part of it, if you aren't involved . . . in some deeper, longer, more significant story?"*

"I watched an Internet video the other day about what people on their deathbeds regretted most," I continued. "You know what it was? All this junk they hadn't gotten around to doing while they were alive! Why hadn't they ever taken a hot-air balloon ride? Why hadn't they visited Antarctica? The guy

202

narrating the video, his whole point was: 'Get out there! Make that great invention! Find that girl of your dreams! Because when it comes time to die, you're going to regret it if you haven't had all these fine adventures.' Now, there's nothing wrong with going out and finding the right girl and going to Antarctica, I guess. But what I found so disturbing about the video was how unquestioningly it accepted the assertion that when your present life is over, your existence as a conscious, unique individual being is over too."

Emerging from this impassioned speech, I took another swig of Red Bull, and continued, in a quieter mode:

"I guess someone, a psychologist looking at me, for example, might say that I just hate endings, probably because my parents divorced when I was very young, you know, all that junk. Well, I know I was affected by my parents' divorce. I know that the interests one has in life have all kinds of findable causes, including personal, psychological ones. But I can't leave it at that. I think my absolute, gut objection to the idea that when we die we're dead and the universe came into being for no real reason—I think its causes run much deeper than all that. I think this feeling exists because something truly deep in me, something absolutely central to who and what I am, simply says: 'No, it isn't true.' And I think there are a lot of other people out there like me—people who have the same basic negative, gut reaction to the vision of pointlessness modern science presents us with."

"Well," said Bernie, "the thing to remember about people like Hawking and Weinberg is that just because they are brilliant at physics doesn't gurantee they know diddlysquat about anything else. Ignoramus is simply Latin for 'we do not know.' They are very good at what they are paid to do—which is basically to figure out how the universe works using mathematics as their primary tool. But they are lousy philosophers. Both of those men are as conversant with the discoveries science has made in recent years as anyone on earth. Yet when they open their mouths to tell you what it all means, what it turns out to mean is, basically, nothing. And that's ironic, because the scientists who came before them—the ones whose shoulders they're standing on—thought differently. Each and every one of them!

"There isn't a single one of the primary architects of relativity theory and quantum mechanics, the two major breakthroughs in physics in the last century, who wasn't deeply interested in the spiritual implications of what they had discovered. And that goes not just for physicists, but for astrophysicists as well. Listen to this," Bernie said, and headed back down to his study again, emerging a few minutes later with another book.

"This is what Arthur Stanley Eddington, arguably the greatest astrophysicist of the first part of the twentieth century, had to say about the physical world that Hawking and Weinberg both feel has such total dominion over us:

" 'It is difficult for the matter-of-fact physicist to accept the view that the substratum of everything is of mental character. But no one can deny that mind is the first and most direct thing in our experience, and all else is remote inference.'[1]

> *"There isn't a single one of the primary architects of relativity theory and quantum mechanics, the two major breakthroughs in physics in the last century, who wasn't deeply interested in the spiritual implications of what they had discovered."*

"'*The substratum of everything is of mental character.*' What an extraordinary sentence! It's not just that, for Eddington, so-called physical reality, the world that we experience directly through our senses, isn't real after all. It's that what truly *is* real is not only nonphysical—it's *mental.*

"What Eddington is really talking about in this sentence is . . . consciousness. Now, the word 'consciousness' is only three hundred years old. And these days, it gets batted around so much, by so many people, for so many different reasons, that it's hard to just stop and sit with that word, and consider what it really means. On a basic level, of course, 'consciousness' means 'awareness,' our ability to know that the world around us is

---

1 Arthur Stanley Eddington, *The Nature of the Physical World.*

there—that it has being, that it *is*. But what lies behind that apparently simple meaning?"

"Well," I said, "I have my ideas. But this book, all the talking I've been doing notwithstanding, is supposed to be about you. So . . . what do you think lies behind it?"

"I think what lies behind it is what James Jeans, the other premier astrophysicist of the first half of the twentieth century, had to say about this apparently physical universe we live in. 'The universe,' he said, 'begins to look more like a great thought than a great machine.'"

If human beings are made in God's image, then all our abilities, from painting to architecture to computer programming, issue from our minds: minds created by God, and thus reflective of his mind. Far from disproving God, the discoveries of every field of science give clues to God's true nature.

Bernie paused, as if to let those words just float in the air for a moment.

"So there you have the two greatest minds in astrophysics at the dawn of this new era we live in, and both are basically saying the same thing: The universe is a *mental* place before it is a physical one. What are we to make of this? Sadly, all too many scientists today, and certainly all too many astrophysicists, want to make nothing of it."

This made sense to me on a number of levels. If human beings are made in God's image, then all our abilities, from painting to architecture to computer programming, issue from our minds: minds created by God, and thus reflective of *his* mind. Far from disproving God, the discoveries of every field of science give clues to God's true nature.

Everything we can do, God can do better. But within the things we *can* do lie clues, endless clues, to what God is really like. We will never be able to completely comprehend God, but with each new ability we develop, each new discovery we make about ourselves and the universe we find ourselves in, we are given another angle, another glimpse, into what God truly is.

> *We will never be able to completely comprehend God, but with each new ability we develop, each new discovery we make about ourselves and the universe we find ourselves in, we are given another angle, another glimpse, into what God truly is.*

CHAPTER 17

Entanglement

Most of Bernie's and my talks that last week had something of a preaching-to-the-choir feel to them. Again and again, I found myself circling the conversation back around to that simple—yet endlessly profound—idea that consciousness was the solid thing, the lasting thing, in the universe. And the more time I spent with this idea, the more I realized that "consciousness" was a word that held within it other words.

Words like "personality," "individuality," "meaning," and "purpose."

For just as the light of the fourth day, the "exterior" light of the sun and moon, came after that other, deeper, more primary light spoken into being by God on the first day, so were all human qualities built upon that initial, all-supporting reality:

the reality of consciousness, which was the true First Thing in God's created world.

Meanwhile, as these lofty insights unfolded on the big brown couch in the living room, I was doing my best to make sure Bernie took his pills and had something to eat at night. Truth be told, back in my days at the house when Marsha was in charge, I had thought she was a little bossy. But now that I was in charge, I saw that Bernie really did need the marshaling that he was always complaining about.

Marsha mothered Bernie, as she had, I suspected, since the beginning of their days together. But at the same time, it was clear that Bernie's absentmindedness was in large part willful. How, after all, could a guy who could multiply two three-digit numbers in his head in just a few seconds be so mentally challenged that he could not remember to take his pills every day? The closest I ever saw him come to forgetting anything in the science department was when he was recalling the date of this or that scientific discovery, the names of the scientists involved, or the atomic number of, say, plutonium. But even in such cases, the answer soon dropped, as from the sky, into his head.

No, Bernie was all there. So when exchanges like the following occurred, I knew that willful absentmindedness, not real forgetfulness, was the culprit.

Me: Bernie, is Pogo still outside?
Bernie (after a short pause, staring straight ahead): Yeah.

Me: It's getting pretty dark. Shouldn't we take her in
  before she gets eaten by a raccoon or something?

Bernie: Yeah.

Me: Um, okay. So where do you think I'd find Pogo if I
  were to go look for her now?

Bernie: Probably the upper-right section of the
  fenced-in garden out back.

And so forth. If I hadn't suggested that Pogo be retrieved,
would Pogo have been doomed to a night outside? I could never
quite tell.

The most impressive exchange of this nature came two days
before my departure from the Haisch household. On the afternoon of the day I was to leave, some of Bernie's family was going
to drive down from San Francisco to celebrate Bernie's birthday.

Me: So Bernie, you've got some relatives coming in two
  days. I figure I'll be some hours gone by the time
  they get here. What's going to happen?

Bernie (noncommittal): Oh, a barbecue.

Me: A barbecue? Like with hamburgers or something?

Bernie: Yeah.

Me: So, um, who's going to get the hamburgers?

Bernie: I guess I am.

Me: Right. Well, tell you what. Suppose I just run over
  to the store and get them now?

Bernie (after a pause): Yeah. That would be great.

Me: So . . . do you think I should get anything else
while I'm there?

Bernie: Hm?

Me: You know. Buns. Ketchup. Um . . . potato chips?

**Bernie (as if running some theorem on star mass
through his head):** Yeah. All that would be good.
Maybe some sauerkraut too.

Thinking about Marsha and Bernie and their likably funny marriage that I'd been given a brief glimpse into, one word kept occurring to me. It was a word that had come up during Bernie's and my discussion of Bell's Theorem, and the way that paired particles had of mirroring each other instantly, no matter their distance.

That word was "entanglement."

Bell's Theorem shows that you can separate two particles that have been made to have a fundamental connection with each other—perhaps by locking them into opposite spins—and you can send them to opposite ends of the galaxy. If one spins one way, the other particle will instantly react to this. This phenomenon destroys the concept of physical space as an ultimate reality, but—like most of science—it also has something to teach us humans as we struggle to navigate this world.

In the Bible there is a lot of talk of two things being of one substance. Eve is of one substance with Adam. Jesus is of one substance with God. If the Bible were being written in the language of modern physics, we could say that both Adam and Eve, and God and Jesus, are entangled.

"Entanglement" sounds like a negative word. People getting divorced certainly use the word in that sense. But in physics, "entanglement" simply means inseparability. Not inseparability in terms of the apparent distance between two particles, which can be enormous. Rather, it means a certain unbreakable closeness that no distance, no apparent isolation, can destroy. There's no getting two particles that are entangled entirely apart. Not because one particle owes the other money, or refuses to grant the other particle a divorce, but because they are of the same substance.

Which boils things down to one question:

What is substance?

Substance, it was starting to seem, is consciousness, because consciousness is the only genuinely substantive thing in the universe, even though we have been trained to think the exact opposite. When people get married, it seemed to me, consciousness needs to be involved. My wife Colleen and I had waited for years for my divorce from my previous wife to go through. We had been married just the previous December, and now we appeared to be hopelessly, and terminally, at odds.

Why, I wondered one night while doing my usual pre-Ambien meditations in Taylor's bed, was the pain one suffered in a breakup with a wife or girlfriend so acute? What, in short, was threatened or damaged by it?

The answer was surprisingly simple. In becoming involved with another person in any kind of serious way, one opened oneself to him or her, and that person, in turn, opened him- or herself to you.

Fine. But what did that really mean? It had been my experience that when you were really in love with someone else, that person took on a sort of transparency. You saw them not as a physical being in the physical world, but as something deeper, and more complex. You might say that the sensation was of seeing that person's whole life, spread out right in front of you. And the other person, in turn, suddenly saw you in this strange, transparent way as well. It was a sort of dual transparency, and in that sharing of one's inner personality, each person revealed to the other the secret of secrets: that we are not just simple physical bodies walking around for a brief and pointless spell, but infinitely larger, infinitely more complex beings, gifted with an infinitely vast, and infinitely complex, future.

When you got married, your own interior was no longer connected to the interior of the other in a passing way, but your entanglement was, as it were, sanctified. And that was why, when you split up with someone, it was as if a bit of yourself was being ripped out. For in fact, that was what was happening.

Woolly and provisional as all these bedtime thoughts were, they drove home to me an idea that I'd been getting more and more excited about in the course of my talks with Bernie. As Bernie made scientific point after scientific point, I kept trying to relate them to ideas I knew from the Gospels. Not because I wanted to come up with some grotesque combination of the Gospels with quantum physics, but because I was, with every passing day, more fascinated by the way one subject mirrored the other without either necessarily being sucked into the other.

Weddings are all over the Gospels. And in the Book of Revelation, when it comes time for John of Patmos to come up with an image for the reunion of man and God, of earth and the heavens, of the healing of the sundering of the human and the divine that had occurred at the Fall, what appears? More images of brides and bridegrooms.

"Scientists," Bernie told me one day on that big, brown seventies couch, "are still struggling to make sense of Bell's Theorem, and of entanglement. That's one reason why I think the computer simulation model of reality is so important. If we could just learn to see this world for what it is—a passing simulation which we, conscious and eternal beings, are moving through momentarily—we could see that in fact, *all* of us are entangled. All of us are, in essence, one body."

"Well," I said, "I'd say that's not an idea science can take credit for." Then, almost as an afterthought, I said:

"If Marsha were here, I bet she'd get all new agey on us and say that what we're really united by is love."

"Well," said Bernie, "I guess that might just be true. But it's a little above my paygrade. I'll stop at consciousness, because as a scientist, I know that consciousness, as the one genuine reality, truly does unite us, and gives us hope. Beyond that, I don't think, is my business."

We are of one body, we are united by love, and we have hope, for we have a future.

I had found my third Key.

CHAPTER 18

Bernie's Proofs

For bernie's and my last interview, I decided to give him a chance to formally present what he saw as his proofs of God. Throughout our talks, I had been assembling my own personal Keys to allowing God back into both the scientific enterprise and—more importantly for me—the enterprise of my own, personal experience of the world.

But Bernie was the scientist, and he was the one who could make this case most persuasively. So for our last talk, I laid things out for him. I was going back East, and was going to assemble things as I saw fit, and make all this stuff I'd experienced, and that we'd talked about, into a book. But it was important that, in all that assembling, Bernie's core thoughts on the matter not be lost.

"So," I said. "The book's called *Proof of God*, and it's going to have your name on it as well as mine. So . . . go for it."

"Well," said Bernie, "there's no point in pretending that we've given any kind of formal logical proof of God's existence. It's not like proving the Pythagorean Theorem in geometry."

"Formal logical proof?" I asked.

"Yes. Formal logic is a specific philosophic discipline, and it proceeds by means of logical proofs following a basic 'if-then' strategy. Kurt Gödel, a famous mathematician and friend of Einstein's, used a very complex and abstract set of propositions to logically prove God's existence. The essence of the argument is that, given the possible existence of any number of worlds, it can be logically shown that a god-like being must exist in all of them. Given that all-powerful beings must share a certain number of attributes, whatever the nature of these hypothetical other worlds may be, it can, ultimately, be shown that there must, logically speaking, be a single all-powerful God who is in charge of all these worlds. Needless to say, Gödel's proof had its critics, but it's interesting to note that Gödel himself very much adhered to it, and that, in the months leading up to his death, he also became convinced that there is a logical proof that the personality survives death. But I confess, I can't follow the many pages of symbolic logic . . . it's beyond me.

"Nevertheless it's all very interesting stuff, but it's probably best to leave those interested in this line of inquiry to read Gödel for themselves. The world of logical proofs is a universe

unto itself, and pretty hard to enter without considerable training. But, on a superficial level, I think it does say something
that a thinker of Gödel's stature could manage to convince not
only others but himself that God can be logically proven, even
if there are always going to be those who develop counterargu-
ments."

"Well," I said, "I guess it's a good idea to tip your hat to all
that, and to let the reader know it's out there. But what say we
get back to the real world?"

"Right," said Bernie, "if I were to give the top, most compelling proofs of God's existence, they would be as follows.

"First, there's the Big Bang itself. It should not be forgotten
how recent this theory is, or how powerful an argument it is for
the existence of a Creator."

"That's interesting," I said. "Here we've been talking about
the Big Bang throughout these conversations, just taking it for
granted. But I know there are a lot of people who hear the words
'Big Bang' and think it suggests just the opposite of God. This is
one of those areas where science and religion seem to be at odds,
at least in the minds of many people."

> *"There's the Big Bang itself. It should not
> be forgotten how recent this theory is, or
> how powerful an argument it is for the
> existence of a Creator."*

"If there's anything that the Big Bang *is not*," said Bernie, "it's evidence *against* God's existence. Though people tend to think it's been around forever, the observation of the remnant radiation from the Big Bang is pretty recent, and has only come to be accepted by a majority of scientists in the last few decades."

"Most scientists do accept it now though, right?"

"Yes," said Bernie. "But that acceptance constitutes a massive change. Before the Big Bang came along, the consensus among scientists was that the universe had existed forever. The idea of an eternally old universe is at least as old as the ancient Greeks, and, among scientists, only started to be questioned in the 1920s. It was then that an astronomer named Edwin Hubble noticed that certain spiral nebulae (that is, galaxies with a thick center and spiral arms, like the one we live in), out at the edge of the then-known universe, had a pronounced redshift in their spectral lines. What was causing this?

"The answer came in 1927, when a Belgian Catholic priest and astronomer named Georges Lemaître suggested that the redshift of these galaxies was a result of the fact that they were moving away from us at tremendous speed. Light waves are shifted toward the long end of the visible spectrum for a galaxy moving away from us, a phenomenon called the Doppler shift.[1] As an object emitting light waves moves away from

---

1 To be precise, this redshifting is due to the stretching of space, which is similar but not the same as Doppler shifting.

us, the waves of light get stretched out. In other words, they get longer, which means that these waves, when they hit our eyes here on earth, look red. Blue shifts, which would indicate motion toward us, were not seen. This was the first hint science got that the universe is expanding.

"Flash forward from the twenties to 1964, when two technicians, Arno Penzias and Robert W. Wilson, were assigned by Bell Labs to eliminate radio static. As you no doubt remember, before radio and television tuning was digital, if you tuned your radio in between stations, you heard static. Likewise, if you clicked your television to an unused channel, you saw what we used to call 'snow'—that is, a flurry of random, staticky dots that created the equivalent of a flickering, grayish, electrical mush. Meanwhile, you could hear a buzzy hiss like what you'd hear on the radio if you tuned between stations.

"So Penzias and Wilson were tasked to come up with a way of eliminating this static. They got rid of some of it, but try as they might they were unable to eliminate it completely. Then they made an extraordinary discovery. In trying to rout out where this static was coming from, they discovered that it appeared to be coming evenly from the entire sky.

"The two scientists eventually received Nobel Prizes, for it turned out that what they had inadvertently stumbled on was the remnant noise, the background radiation, left over from the Big Bang.

"This was a huge cosmological discovery, but as interesting as it was for astrophysics, it was an even bigger discovery in terms of the God/no God argument.

"Genesis, of course, maintains that the universe was created all at once by God, and before the Big Bang Theory came along it was common practice to use this fact as evidence *against* the existence of God. Back when it was assumed that the universe was infinitely old and infinitely large, the notion that it was suddenly created, as in Genesis, seemed preposterous. How could time and space possibly have a beginning?

"But lo and behold, we now find ourselves living in a world that did indeed have a beginning, some 13.7 billion years ago. By extrapolating from the fact that the universe is expanding, as it unquestionably is, astrophysicists have rewound the tape, as it were. Using mathematical and physical strategies that we can't go into here, but that you can read about in books like Steven Weinberg's *The First Three Minutes*, it has been established that the universe 'exploded' out of a point-like, multimillion-degree 'thing' called a singularity, which contained all the energy in the universe to be. This is about as strong a validation of the theological concept of *creatio ex nihilo*, or 'creation out of nothing,' as you could ask for. It also can't be stressed enough that before the remarkable series of discoveries and calculations that led to ratification of the Big Bang Theory, conventional science essentially laughed at this idea: to the point that even the originator of the term 'Big Bang' (Fred Hoyle) came up with the term Big Bang, essentially, as a joke.

"This brings us to what I would say is my number two proof:

the one we spent a good part of the last week discussing. That is, the finely tuned nature of the universe. Though we spent a lot of time discussing some of the more impressive examples of just how finely tuned it is, we didn't get into how and when the idea first entered discussion.

> *Hoyle made the famous comparison between claiming life arose on earth by accident and claiming a tornado would blow through a junkyard and produce a Boeing 747.*

"One benchmark came in 1961, when a physicist named Robert Dicke proposed that certain forces in physics needed to be fine-tuned for life to exist. Some twenty years later, a very respected cosmologist named Sir Fred Hoyle, mentioned above, advanced this argument further in his 1984 book *Intelligent Universe*. Hoyle made the famous comparison between claiming life arose on earth by accident and claiming a tornado would blow through a junkyard and produce a Boeing 747.

"Then came John Gribbin and Martin Rees, who published a defense of the fine-tuning argument in their 1989 book, *Cosmic Coincidences*. Since then, the topic has become a popular one, and there have been a number of books, like the one you like, Strobel's *The Case for a Creator*, that try and bring some of this stuff far enough down to earth that ordinary readers can grasp it.

"NASA launched the Kepler Observatory, an unmanned super-telescope that circles the sun, in March 2009. Its specific purpose was to seek out stars that are circled by planets similar to ours.

"Hopes were high that the telescope would uncover at least some such planetary systems. Why? The more such systems were found, the greater likelihood that there might be life elsewhere in our universe.

"To say that some such planetary systems were discovered is an understatement. The results were stunning, and took almost everyone by surprise. As of April of this year (2017), nearly 2,500 'exoplanets' (planets orbiting stars other than our sun) have been detected. If we take the Kepler results and extrapolate from them—that is, if we ask what the implications of this 'local' discovery are for the possibility of life elsewhere in the Milky Way and beyond it, in other galaxies, we discover a universe that is stunningly well-crafted to support life.

"But just to stick to our own galaxy: Astronomers estimate that there should be one hundred billion planets in our home galaxy that we know as the Milky Way. How many, if any, support life? We of course don't know. But here's what we *do* know: The amount of planetary systems with a generally 'life-friendly' profile far exceeds what we would expect to find in a universe that arose randomly, with no 'agenda' to produce life.

"To create a universe with such a large number of planetary

systems potentially capable of supporting life, certain criteria need to be met.

"First off, we need an expanding universe that is expanding at *just the right speed* to allow ordinary matter, dark matter, and dark energy to form. Remember: the universe expands a little too fast, then no livable planets. A little too slow, then again, no livable planets. (In fact, most likely no universe at all.) Our universe is expanding at precisely the right speed to make planet formation likely.

"But not only do we need a universe in which dark matter, dark energy, regular energy, regular matter and, of course, planets, can form: We also need a universe capable of allowing for the formation of galaxies. Things happen slowly in our universe. Without a relatively undisturbed stretch of, say, ten million years, planets wouldn't have a chance to form, and life wouldn't have a chance to take hold and grow. The initial stars in the universe need just the right kind of gas and dust to form out of. The planets circling those stars have to have favorable (read: very stable) conditions for life to develop, and they need to have plenty of carbon, because carbon is the building block of life.

"Over the past thirty or so years, it has become increasingly obvious that the universe shows extraordinarily strong signs of being 'set up' so that just such objectives could be met. Laws— like the strength of the force of gravity or the force of electricity (for electricity has been 'set' at a certain strength too) were established for our universe before the universe took shape. And the exactitude at which those dials were set, as it were, are so exact that no one—not even mathematicians—have the mental capability to fully grasp them. Their exactitude is too huge.

"Ironically, even Stephen Hawking talks about this. In *A Brief History of Time*, Hawking writes: 'The laws of science, as we know them at present, contain many fundamental numbers, like the size of the electric charge of the electron and the ratio of the masses of the proton and the electron. . . . The remarkable fact is that the values of these numbers seem to have been very finely adjusted to make possible the development of life.'

"Hawking has as good a grasp of just how extraordinary the level of fine-tuning in the universe is as anyone alive, and he is the first to admit that these numbers are in need of an explanation. But . . . he simply refuses to acknowledge the most obvious one. The physicist David Darling said of Hawking: 'He may be a genius, but his opinions about God carry no more weight than those of his next-door neighbor.' That little gem of wisdom is worth keeping in mind.

"This leads us to the third proof. In their book *The Grand Design*, Stephen Hawking and Leonard Mlodinow draw an important distinction between reality and models of reality. The world is a complicated and messy place. The only way to get a handle on certain aspects of how it works is to create a model of it. But . . . models can only attain a certain level of complexity. Take the weather, for example. If we could build a big enough model of the earth's weather patterns—one that took in sufficiently exact data on temperature, humidity, and other relevant variables for every cubic inch of atmosphere . . . well, we would never have to worry about whether the evening news was going to get the next day's weather right, because they'd get it right every time. Unfortunately, building that big a model just isn't feasible.

"The same goes for reality itself. Today it is possible to have a frighteningly realistic experience of living in another world in a game called Avatars. A huge number of interacting players worldwide can participate. It will not be long before we can plug ourselves into a super-hyper computer capable of rendering fantastically real landscapes that we can participate in so deeply that it will feel one hundred percent real.

"You were put off when I started talking about these developments," Bernie said. "But then, I hope, you came to understand why I find them so compelling. These games are models, on a very small level, of the reality that we are actually living in right now. You asked some days back if I think we are in a giant video game, and my answer is, basically, yes. We are beings of consciousness. We are real. And the universe we are living in is a simulation made by God specifically to allow us to be alive in it. So to say it once again, the birth of computer simulation technology has given us a hint, but hint enough, for us to get a grasp of what this world around us really is. It's an illusion, but a brilliant, dazzling, and deeply purposeful one. The revolution in computer-simulated realities has given us a model—not a perfect one, but a pretty darn good one—for how God simulates the apparent reality in which we find ourselves. It's a simulation composed, ultimately, by consciousness. How can consciousness create a rock? The answer to that is simple: There *are* no real rocks. Material reality is an illusion. A very, very good one, but it was made by God, so we would expect it to be pretty well done. In the end, simulations are all just a matter of two things: consciousness and numbers. That is, mathematics. That's what computer simulations are, and that's what this simulation we're sitting in right now is: real immortal spiritual beings clothed in simulated bodies and living in a simulated reality.

"Bear in mind, I am not claiming that God is some vast electronic computer somewhere. I am proposing that he can create virtual realties with his thoughts. He can create and run a program that is the universe, so to speak, using his mind and thoughts.

"Why is this a third proof of God? Because elaborate computer simulations call for a programmer, just as the existence of laws call for a creator of those laws. It is my belief—and very close to my certainty—that this fantastically elaborate dream we are currently living in was created, not by some bored thirteen-year-old sitting on some futuristic couch years from now, but by God. I would say that the model of God as a great consciousness creating virtual worlds for his offspring to live and evolve in solves the problem of the great how and the great why . . . at least at the fifty-thousand-foot level view . . . or maybe the hundred-thousand-foot level. I would add this to the list of things that I think add up to proof.

"Now, to this we could add many other arguments for God's existence. The moral dimension, for one. Why do people have an innate sense of goodness?

"These are arguments for the existence of a world of realities stretching beyond the simply physical. And we are after bigger game than that. My view is that we have conclusive evidence for it, and that if this were any other kind of problem, scientists would be unanimous in their agreement that we have proof. But this is, as we know, not just any old subject. So these proofs are ignored, even though it is, in my mind, entirely unscientific to do so."

CHAPTER 19

The Light

W HEN I GOT back to Nyack, I checked into the Time Hotel
again, and for the first time really appreciated the irony of its
name. A hotel called the Time, with a skull as its logo, with
rooms that looked out onto a cemetery. Life really did have an
odd way of slipping meaning into things, just when they seemed
at their most meaningless.

This time around, however, I was given a room on the other
side of the hotel—the side that looked onto 287, the highway
that funneled drivers over the Tappan Zee Bridge into West-
chester and beyond. This room, unlike the first one, where I'd
spent that miserable month at the beginning of the summer,
had a porch, and sitting out on it in the mornings, I'd watch
the cars whoosh past toward the Tappan Zee the way someone

might watch a flowing river. You never, said the Greek philosopher Heraclitus, step into the same river twice, and though a lot
of that philosopher's sayings were cryptic, that one wasn't. The
world around us changes constantly, that's what Heraclitus was
saying. Everything is flowing sand.

But not quite everything. For in truth, the being who looks
out at the flowing sand is looking from a place he cannot recognize, because he has his back to it. We are born with our backs
toward God, and come to know him not by turning around, but
by turning, as Jesus himself counsels us to do, within. When we
do, we see that everything comes from Him. Not just the passing world before us, but we ourselves, the beings looking out
upon that world, and wondering on it.

Bernie is a man who speaks with the utmost caution about
what he knows, and is more than ready to lay out what he doesn't
know. The sciences, I continue to believe, should have more Ber-
nies in them. Because science is, at this great crisis point of faith,
exactly what we need. A bit of basic knowledge of what physics has uncovered in the last hundred or so years is far from a
deterrent to belief. Instead, it is something that spurs us toward it.
Science tells us the universe is a place of intense purpose: a place
from which God has partially removed Himself, so that possibility (including, most importantly and problematically, free will)
may unfold. As beings fashioned by God, we carry bodies made
of stardust, and a consciousness that transcends all physical matter and links us directly to our maker. We are here for a reason.

*A bit of basic knowledge of what physics has
uncovered in the last hundred or so years
is far from a deterrent to belief. Instead,
it is something that spurs us toward it.
Science tells us the universe is a place of
intense purpose: a place from which God
has partially removed Himself, so that
possibility (including, most importantly
and problematically, free will) may unfold.*

Perfectly baked blueberry pies do not just appear on countertops. It is as simple, and as fantastically, wonderfully complex, as that.

After a few days at the Time Hotel, I collected some possessions from Colleen's house and drove up to Islesboro, that same island off the coast of Maine where I'd spent my childhood summers. My sister and brother-in-law had a summer house that had been winterized, where they said I was welcome to stay. I got to work on this book, and in the afternoons I took long walks down to the end of the island, to the same spot I'd visited when I was a child, and then a teenager.

On either side of the road, the rocks were unchanged from how they'd been when I'd looked at them as a ten-year-old, a fifteen-year-old, and then a twenty-year-old.

But while the rocks were the same, I had changed considerably. I'd put on weight, my lungs were less than what they once were, thanks to all the cigarettes I'd smoked in my twenties and thirties, and my head was crowded full of all sorts of life experiences: losses and gains, confusions and clarities . . . a parade of things good and bad that I was glad I hadn't known were coming at me when I was fifteen.

Most of the time on these walks, I listened to music on the same iPhone I'd used to record Bernie's and my talks. For reasons unknown, I found myself listening almost exclusively to Led Zeppelin, and in particular to "Stairway to Heaven."

How, I wondered, was it possible for someone like me, a male American born in 1962, who had certainly heard "Stairway to Heaven" somewhere in the neighborhood of ten thousand times, to be able to play it, again and again, as I took that two-hour walk down to the end of the island and back?

When I got to the tip of the island, I usually hit the beach around the time that the sun—a sun I had spent a lot of time thinking about that summer—was nearing the horizon, sinking below the pines on an island just across the water called, amusingly enough to me, Job Island.

All around me, the rocks I'd known since I was a child lit up with that strange, dense, super-orange light that the sun gives off just before it sets.

One day, watching this show, I realized why it was that I was able to listen to "Stairway to Heaven" with such fresh ears, despite having heard it so many times over my life. Toward the end of the song, Robert Plant talks about things turning to gold, and how, if one listens hard enough, one will find the tune—the tune that, in the song, is a metaphor for the reason one is alive.

I was listening to "Stairway to Heaven" again and again because finding the tune, and things turning, in the end, to gold, was what my summer—and the book I was now going to try to write—were all about.

My situation with Colleen was still a mess, my future was uncertain, and I was, at that point, still struggling to put together what my summer spent in Bernie's company had meant. But despite all these problems, I knew, somehow, that the aquarium I swam in, the field of existence I was immersed in at all times, had become larger. Or, rather, it had revealed itself to have been larger the whole time.

On the days when the golden light from the about-to-set sun was especially strong, and the beach and the trees and the rocks and everything around me really turned to gold, I was able to see that light for what it really was: an earthly reflection of another, higher light. The light which the Gospel of John calls the light of all men, and which it describes as shining in the darkness: a darkness that, however often that it seems it might, does not overcome it.

The story of material things is never, in the end, a happy one. Shipwreck awaits every last piece of the material world. In the end, there is nothing solid, nothing firm enough to hold on to.

Yet solidity exists. In this world of passing shades and shadows, of loss and disillusionment, something isn't lost, something doesn't disappoint, something doesn't fade away to nothing. The Bible calls this mysterious something the "light of men," and says that it is consoling. Why is this light consoling? The Gospel of John is clear on this. Because darkness does not overcome it. This darkness has many synonyms, especially today. Separation. Alienation. Ignorance. Loneliness. Sadness. Violence. Dishonesty. Discord. All these and more fall under the cloak of the "darkness" that the New Testament speaks of, just as all manner of words fall under the cloak of the "light" that overcomes it. Unity. Return. And above all, love. The darkness is the darkness of the superficial world, which is that of separation. The light that overcomes it is the true light of all men, which is the light of return. Of unity. Of the conquest of all apparent separation. The light of God.

By the time I turned around and headed back toward the empty house where I was working on this book, the light, the golden light that, minutes before, had seemed like it would never go away, was gone. The familiar rock formations that I'd passed on the way to the beach were no longer glowing and alive, but indistinct, vaguely sinister shapes, humped in darkness.

But I was not fooled. I was solid. The people I loved, the people who came in and out of my life . . . they were solid as well. The emotions I felt, those seemingly most fleeting and flimsy things, were solid too. And the rock-hard, rough-and-tumble world around me, the one I had been struggling through for fifty-four years—that world was not solid, all appearances to the contrary. It was a quantum illusion—a dance of energy in particulate form that my brain was trained to read as solid and substantial, but which in fact was the furthest thing imaginable from these qualities.

I had now spent enough time with Bernie, and spent enough time bending my brain over the Zero Point Field and computer analogies and whatever else, to pick up the essential point—the third Key on that mental key chain that I had been looking, and hoping, to find. Love is real. Personality is real. Human experience, good and bad, is real. Human beings, as C. S. Lewis once boldly put it, will outlive the universe. The digitized rocks and trees around me would fall away, because they weren't made of anything to begin with. But the place at the very center of myself, the place not outside me but deep within me, so deep and so central that it was impossible to see because it was where seeing itself came from . . . that would not fall away. It would not because it was, and always had been, a gift—a pure gift from the God who created this far-from-random cosmos—given out of pure generosity, with no strings attached.

One day in Maine, while I was trying to get this book into shape and taking my walks down to the end of the island and timing my walks so that I could watch the sun, the star that was responsible for the earth, and for my being there on the earth, watching it with eyes made with materials forged within other, long-dead, faraway stars. (In the simulation model of reality, astrophysical processes are, of course, a simulation.) On one of those days, Bernie called and asked how the book was doing.

"Oh," I said, "it's coming together."

But of course, that wasn't quite the case. In the real world, nothing just comes together. From books, to universes, to blueberry pies, a little extra help is always needed.

PTOLEMY'S THREE KEYS

1. *The physical world is not real. It is not substantive. It feels that way, and it looks that way, but it isn't. There's nothing in it, because there's no such thing as solid matter.*

2. *Consciousness is the only reality in our universe. Matter, energy, space . . . All these things are only simulations, generated by God using the sole and single "thing" in this universe that actually exists. The world of objects we move through is not conscious, but we are. And because we are conscious, we are real.*

3. *Love is real and connects us all.*

ACKNOWLEDGMENTS

Ptolemy Tompkins: In addition to Bernie and Marsha, without whose enthusiasm and hospitality this book would never have been, I'd like to thank my longtime mentor and friend Stephan Schwartz for introducing Bernie and me, Jonathan Merkh at Howard Books, our stupendous editor Beth Adams, my agents Art Klebanoff and Jen Gates (along with everyone else at Aevitas Creative). Thanks to Rick Willett, for his fine copyediting, and Chris Milea, for his production editing. Thanks to Kate Farrell, Bill Manning, all the Trains (especially Maria Teresa and Francie, Sue Townsend, Karl Taro Greenfeld, Mara Lieber, Elliott Goldkind, Mary Belton, Oliver Ray, Jean Lenihan, Isreal Segal, Richard Ryan, Terrence Patrick McGovern, Jerry Smith, Greg Mirhej, Christie Ray Robb, Leeza Mangaldas, the brilliant Steve Sittenreich, Alix Thorne, Arch and Linda Gillies, Richard Smoley, Mitch Horowitz, Mark Booth, Gary Lachman, Christina Johnstone, the ever-patient Samantha Manning, Colleen Hughes, Lulu Scherman,

Evie Scherman, and last but very much not least, my sister, Robin.

Bernard Haisch: I acknowledge the collegial support of Prof. Alfonso Rueda, Dr. Hal Puthoff, Prof. Garret Model, Prof. Peter Sturrock, Prof. Robert Jahn, Brenda Dunne, Dr. Larry Dossey, the late Prof. Ian Stevenson, Russell Targ. Prof. Rudy Schild, Prof. Eric Priest, Prof. Peter Ulmschneider, Prof. Owen Gingerich, Prof. Arnold Benz, Prof. Richard Henry, and Prof. Stephen Post. I also recognize the Society for Scientific Exploration for its support of frontier science. I wish to thank the monks of the Bhaktivedanta Institute in Calcutta, India, for inviting me to speak and share perspectives on these topics.

Thanks to Stephan Schwartz for introducing me to my co-author, Ptolemy Tompkins.

I owe special thanks to Dr. Tom Campbell, author of My Big TOE (Theory of Everything) for introducing me to the concept of evolving digital consciousness in virtual realities. He is on the right path.

Finally, major thanks go to our editor, Beth Adams.

APPENDIX

The Three Stooges Explain Heisenberg's Uncertainty Principle (excerpted from *The Purpose-Guided Universe*)

An Ideal Quantum Experiment

Let's examine a quantum experiment devised by three preeminent geniuses of theoretical physics: Dr. Moe, Dr. Larry, and Prof. Curly.

Prof. Curly has devised machines that slice or chop pennies in half. A "slice" is a cut lengthwise through a penny, so that we wind up with two thin coins. One has the profile of Abraham Lincoln on one side and nothing on the back. The other coin has the Lincoln memorial on one side and nothing on the back. This is shown in Figure A.

Sliced   Chopped

Figure A

A "chop" divides the coin in half very differently, resulting in two "half-moon" pennies. One coin has Lincoln's head; the other has Lincoln's shoulders.

Prof. Curly, being the genius that he is, has two versions of the slicing and chopping machine. One is a classical model and one a quantum model.

In experiment one, Prof. Curly uses the classical machine to slice the penny. The machine, being quite sophisticated, puts one sliced coin in one envelope addressed to Dr. Moe, one in another addressed to Dr. Larry, and labels both envelopes "Sliced." Prof. Curly takes the envelopes out of the machine and puts them out for the mailman to pick up. He then goes to take a nap.

The next day Dr. Moe, who lives in Stoogeburg, and Dr. Larry, who lives a hundred miles away in Stoogeville, both get envelopes in the mail. Dr. Moe expects to find a sliced penny inside since that is how the envelope is labeled. He opens his and sure enough, there is a sliced coin inside and it has the Lincoln profile on it. He calls his colleague Dr. Larry, who was still asleep, and sure enough, when he gets his envelope out of the mailbox it contains the backside of the original coin: the Lincoln Memorial.

Dr. Moe calls Prof. Curly and yells at him: "Listen, puddin' head, what kind of silly experiment was that? I got half a coin and Larry got the other half. What does that prove?" To which Prof. Curly responds: "Nyuk, nyuk, nyuk . . . you ain't seen nothin' yet."

In experiment two, Prof. Curly sets the classical machine to "chop." Once again the machine goes to work, turns out two 'half-moon' shaped coins, and puts one in each of two envelopes labeled "Chopped" addressed to Dr. Moe and Dr. Larry.

The next day Dr. Moe finds an envelope labeled "Chopped" in his mailbox. Expecting to find a chopped penny inside, sure enough he discovers one with Lincoln's head. He calls his colleague Dr. Larry, who is busy fixing flapjacks for breakfast. Dr. Larry checks his mailbox, finds an envelope labeled "Chopped," and inside there is the other half of the coin with Lincoln's shoulders.

Dr. Moe calls Prof. Curly and yells: "Oh, a wise guy, eh? What kind of silly experiment was that? I oughta punch . . ." Prof. Curly stops him: "Wait till you see this next one."

It's time for experiment three. This time Prof. Curly fires up the quantum machine. He inserts a coin in the machine. It hums and whirrs and then spits out two sealed envelopes. This time, though, the envelopes are not labeled "Sliced" or "Chopped." Instead they are labeled "Quantum." The mailman picks them up.

The next day Dr. Moe finds an envelope labeled "Quantum" in his mailbox. Just then Prof. Curly calls up.

Curly: Hey, Moe. Did you get the quantum envelope I sent you?

Moe: Yeah, and I'm about to open it.

Curly: Don't do that yet. First you've got to decide whether the envelope contains a sliced or a chopped coin.

Moe: Are you nuts? Your machine already sliced or chopped it. I can't change that now.

Curly: Yes, you can. In fact you've got to decide which one it is to complete the experiment.

Moe: Look here, puddin' head. Are you claiming that if I decide the envelope contains a sliced coin, I'll find that inside, and if I decide it's a chopped coin I'll find that inside?

Curly: That's right.

Moe: Listen here. That's crazy. That would mean that whatever is inside is not quite real.

Curly: Nyuk, nyuk, nyuk.

Moe: All right. I say I'm going to find a chopped coin in there. Now can I also decide which half of the coin I'll find? Lincoln's head or Lincoln's shoulders?

Curly: No. That's the part you have to discover. Looking to see which one it is, is called the measurement. You get to decide which kind of coin you're going to observe, sliced or chopped, but once you've decided that, then chance determines which half it is.

Dr. Moe decides he will find a chopped coin. He then opens the envelope, and just as he decided, there is a half-moon shaped chopped coin. It turns out to be the Lincoln head half. But now he is confused.

Moe: Okay, wise guy, it was a chopped coin. But what about the envelope you sent to Dr. Larry? What if he decides his other half is a sliced coin? That would *not* be the other half of this one?

Curly: It's too late for him to do that. Once you've decided which kind of coin you've got, that fixes the outcome in his envelope. He's going to get the correct other half and he can't change that if you decided first.

Dr. Moe calls Dr. Larry, who was just watching a rerun of *The Three Stooges* on TV. When Dr. Larry opens his envelope, sure enough, it is a chopped coin of Lincoln's shoulders.

Moe: Fiddlesticks. You just got lucky. Let's do this again a few more times.

Curly: Soitanly, nyuk, nyuk, nyuk.

APPENDIX

Needless to say, each time the experiment is done, Dr. Moe finds just the right kind of coin, sliced or chopped, always corresponding to his decision before opening his envelope. And Dr. Larry, who always opens his envelope second, always has the matching half.

SUGGESTED FURTHER READING

1. *The Conscious Universe: The Scientific Truth of Psychic Phenomena*, Dean Radin, HarperOne, 2009.

2. *Consciousness Beyond Life: The Science of the Near-Death Experience*, Pim van Lommel, HarperCollins, 2010.

3. *The Cosmic Landscape: String Theory and the Illusion of Intelligent Design*, Leonard Susskind, Little, Brown and Company, 2005.

4. *Did Jesus Exist? The Historical Argument for Jesus of Nazareth*, Bart D. Ehrman, HarperOne, 2013.

5. *Farewell to Reality: How Modern Physics has Betrayed the Search for Scientific Truth*, Jim Baggott, Pegasus Books, 2014.

6. *A Fortunate Universe: Life in a Finely Tuned Cosmos*, Geraint F. Lewis and Luke A. Barnes, Cambridge University Press, 2016.

7. *God and the Big Bang: Harmony Between Science and Spirituality*, 2nd ed., Daniel C. Matt, Jewish Lights, 2016.

8. *The God Theory*, Bernard Haisch, Weiser Books, 2009.

9. *God? Very Probably.* Robert H. Nelson, Cascade Books, 2015.

10. *The Grand Design*, Stephen Hawking and Leonard Mlodinow, Bantam, 2010.

11. *Is God a Mathematician?* Mario Livio, Simon & Schuster, 2010.

12. *The Lightness of Being: Mass, Ether, and the Unification of Forces,* Frank Wilczek, Basic Books, 2010.

13. *My Big TOE (Theory of Everything)*, Tom Campbell, Lightning Strike Books, 2007.

14. *One Mind: How Our Individual Mind Is Part of a Greater Consciousness and Why It Matters*, Larry Dossey, Hay House, Inc., 2014.

15. *Our Mathematical Universe: My Quest for the Ultimate Nature of Reality*, Max Tegmark, Vintage, 2015.

16. *The Perennial Philosophy*, Aldous Huxley, Harper Perennial Modern Classics, 2009.

17. *The Physics of Christianity*, Frank J. Tipler, Doubleday Religion, 2007.

18. *The Purpose-Guided Universe: Believing in Einstein, Darwin, and God*, Bernard Haisch, New Page Books, 2010.

19. *Quantum Enigma: Physics Encounters Consciousness*, Second Edition, Bruce Rosenblum and Fred Kuttner, Oxford University Press, 2011.

20. *Quantum Physics and Theology: An Unexpected Kinship*, John Polkinghorne, Yale University Press, 2008.

21. *Signposts to God: How Modern Physics & Astronomy Point the Way to Belief*, Peter Bussey, IVP Academic, 2016.

22. *Supernormal: Science, Yoga, and the Evidence for Extraordinary Psychic Abilities*, Dean Radin, Deepak Chopra Books, 2013.

23. *Surviving Death: A Journalist Investigates Evidence for an Afterlife*, Leslie Kean, Crown Archetype, 2017.

24. *There is a God: How the World's Most Notorious Atheist Changed His Mind*, Anthony Flew, HarperOne, 2008.

25. *Time Reborn: From the Crisis in Physics to the Future of the Universe*, Lee Smolin, Mariner Books, 2014.

26. *The Trouble with Physics: The Rise of String Theory, the Fall of Science, and What Comes Next*, Lee Smolin, Mariner Books, 2007.

27. *UFOs: Generals, Pilots, and Government Officials Go on the Record*, Leslie Kean, Three Rivers Press, 2011.

28. *You are the Universe*, Deepak Chopra and Menas Kafatos, Harmony, 2017.